Thorburn's Mammals

Thorburn's Mammals

With an Introduction by David Attenborough
and Notes by Iain Bishop

Ebury Press and Michael Joseph Limited
London

Published in Great Britain by
Ebury Press
Chestergate House,
Vauxhall Bridge Road
London SW1   and
Michael Joseph Limited
52 Bedford Square
London WC1

Illustrations and text by Archibald Thorburn,
first published 1920–1 in *British Mammals*
This edition © George Rainbird Ltd 1974

ISBN 0 7181 1232 6

This book was designed and produced by
Rainbird Reference Books Limited
Marble Arch House, 44 Edgware Road, London W2
House Editor: Perry Morley
Text filmset by Jarrold & Sons Limited, Norwich, England
Printed by Ben Johnson Limited, York, England

Contents

The Latin names used by Thorburn were not always correct. Some reclassification has also taken place since his day. We therefore give more commonly used modern taxonomic names in brackets after the names used by Thorburn. Additional information on classification will be found in the Appendix.

Introduction
by David Attenborough

ARCHIBALD THORBURN died less than forty years ago. Yet he was a direct link with those great artists who, during the second half of the nineteenth century, produced some of the most sumptuous folios of bird plates ever published. The tradition in Britain began at the very end of the eighteenth century when the Newcastle wood engraver, Thomas Bewick, produced his exquisite *History of British Birds* and it reached its apogee with John Gould's magnificent publications.

Part of the appeal of those great books is that the reader feels a direct relationship with the artist. Bewick cut lines on a wood block, put it in a press and inked it. The page in his finished book was thus once in physical contact with that cut line. John Gould – or rather his illustrators, for Gould himself employed others to make finished drawings after his rough designs – drew with a wax pencil on a lithographic stone. That, too, was inked and printed directly. So were the earliest published plates that Thorburn produced.

Thorburn first made his name in 1887 and did so dramatically, rather like a young opera singer who becomes a star overnight by taking over from an indisposed prima donna. J. G. Keulemans, one of the bird artists of the great period and a younger contemporary of Gould, had been engaged by Lord Lilford to provide the illustrations for his *Coloured Figures of the Birds of the British Islands*. But before he was properly launched upon it, he fell ill. To replace him Lilford brought in the twenty-six-year-old Thorburn. Over the next thirteen years, Thorburn produced 268 plates, well over half in Lilford's huge compilation. If anything, they outshine the older man's work in the elegance of their design and the delicacy of their execution.

The particular technique Thorburn used was chromolithography. Looking at those plates, you can still almost feel the mark of his crayon. In the estimate of many, Lilford's *Birds* was the last great bird book in the grand manner. By 1915, when Thorburn came to publish his own *British Birds*, the first book in which he provided both text and plates, things in the printing trade had changed. It was by responding to those changes that he produced books that founded a quite new tradition.

His illustrations in *British Birds* are reproduced by colour halftone, a method that is dependent upon photography. No longer is the impress of his finger palpable on each printed plate. Indeed, in many cases the finished reproductions are not even the same size as his original drawings. It is undoubtedly a loss. But the new technique also brought new qualities. Quite apart from its cheapness and the fact that it made very large editions possible – features that doubtless endeared it to publishers – it also gave the artist new freedoms. In preparing his originals, he could use whatever medium he liked. Oil or watercolour, the halftone plate could reproduce it with delicacy and fidelity. Thorburn took full advantage of these new possibilities both in *British Birds* and in this work, *British Mammals*, which began publication in parts five years later in 1920. As you can see, his pictures here are neither engraved nor drawn with a crayon. They are painted. The thin delicate line of his brush, the deliberate spatter of a coarse stroke, are all visible and a delight. They reveal his sensibilities and perceptions in a new and different way.

But *British Mammals*, while it foreshadows technically the kind of illustrations that have appeared in bird books ever since, still draws elements of its style from the past. Birds are not easy to anthropomorphise. They do not have the right features. It is difficult to make a beak smile. Even the Victorians at their most sentimental only really succeeded by putting them in a human context – a robin bringing a sprig of holly for Christmas, or woodland birds preparing a counterpane of flowers for Hansel and Gretel. But there is no difficulty in humanising mammals. The drooping posture of a dog sitting on his master's grave, the long-nosed grin of a fox, the big eyes and snub nose of a baby rabbit, all can easily be portrayed in a way that underlines in human terms their soulfulness, cunning and innocence. It is a style that, at its worst, is unbearably cloying. A few years ago, when scientific asceticism made it unforgivable to draw any parallel whatsoever between animals and man, such sentimentalism was anathema. Today, perhaps, we are a little more lenient, a little more willing to concede that all human parallels are not totally unjustified. Today, after all, you can even suggest that you admire Landseer's *Monarch of the Glen* and not be greeted with universal mockery. Thorburn, to my eye, has retained some part of this intuitive sympathy with mammals but manages to convey it in a restrained, charming and totally acceptable way. The hedgehog on Plate 7 does seem to be related to Mrs Tiggywinkle, and yet it remains firmly a real hedgehog and, what is more, a scientifically accurate one.

Accuracy was very important to Thorburn. He was, after all, a scientific illustrator. His books, whether in their original form or indeed in this new edition, were designed to help his readers identify the creatures they came across and to visualise those they had not yet seen. How does *British Mammals* stand up by that criterion? The taxonomy of mammals has, of course, been revised since his day. Britain's complement has also changed. Happily, we have not lost any species since his time. Indeed we have gained several that either were not here at all when he wrote, or were so rare that he could ignore them – the grey squirrel, the coypu, the mink, the edible dormouse and various species of deer. But apart from these inevitable consequences of the passage of time, his paintings are remarkably accurate, not only in the way they portray the anatomy but, equally importantly and perhaps more difficult to achieve with veracity and honesty, the personality of each species as a living animal. I suspect that it will be for that exceptional combination of qualities that this work will continue to be valued for a long time to come.

Editor's Note

In this new edition, we have reproduced from the 1920–1 edition all of Thorburn's watercolour plates and the text in its entirety except for a few references to monochrome drawings, which have been deleted since the drawings themselves are not shown. In a few places the order in which the species are discussed in the original text has been slightly rearranged so that each species description appears on the page opposite the relevant plate. These changes are shown in the list on page 120. Occasionally, where one species is shown on two plates, the relevant part of the text is repeated opposite the second plate to save unnecessary turning of pages.

The animals on Thorburn's original plates were drawn reduced in size, as indicated by the figures shown beside the species names. For this edition the plates have been reduced by 1/2 and figures given should therefore be multiplied by 1/2. For example, a figure of 1/3 should now read 1/6; 2/3 should read 1/3; 1/7 should read 1/14; 1/8 should read 1/16.

Author's Preface

THE INTENTION IN ARRANGING THIS WORK has been to provide pictures in colour of all those animals classed as mammals which inhabit or visit our islands.

Planned as a companion to the volumes on *British Birds* and *A Naturalist's Sketch Book*, recently published, it gives a series of reproductions from watercolour drawings of the seventy species which make up the list, and in addition to these are shown various subspecies or closely allied forms, among others some of the local races of mice which have attracted the attention of naturalists during recent years.

Though lacking the brilliant colouring and wonderful singing powers of birds, the four-footed creatures of our fields, woods, and moorlands have each their own charm and attractiveness, from the tiny Harvest Mouse to the wild Red Deer; and as many of them only walk by night, it is no easy task to study their life and habits.

The list of British Mammals is short compared with the much larger number of our native birds; this has allowed more freedom and space in the arrangement of the pictures and enabled me to devote a whole Plate, and occasionally two, to show to advantage some of the more interesting species.

The animals represented belong to the six following orders, namely, twelve Cheiroptera (Bats), five Insectivora (Insect-eating mammals), fifteen Carnivora (Flesh-eating mammals), fourteen Rodentia (Rodents or Gnawing mammals), four Ruminantia (Ruminating mammals), and twenty Cetacea (Whales, Porpoises, Dolphins).

It is not without regret that I have been unable to include pictures of those fine extinct 'beasts of the forest', such as the Wolf, the Wild Boar, Giant Fallow Deer, and others, but in order to keep the volumes within a reasonable size and cost, I have had to content myself with little more than a list of the species which have vanished; this will be found at the end of the second volume [on page 10 of this edition – Ed.].

Until the late Professor Bell published his *British Quadrupeds*, including the Cetacea, in 1837, little was known of the life history of our wild animals, and even then the knowledge of the Bats, Seals and Whales was comparatively meagre; though a great deal of new and reliable information was supplied in the last edition of that work in 1874.

Since then many notable books and treatises on the subject have been written by various authorities, including among other names of repute those of Sir William Flower, Mr J. G. Millais, Major Barrett-Hamilton, Mr J. E. Harting, Mr Oldfield Thomas, Richard Lydekker, Sir Harry Johnston, R. F. Tomes, E. R. Alston, Dr W. Eagle Clarke, Mr T. A. Coward, Mr Lionel Adams, etc.

A short description of the animals represented has been included, giving the general distribution, colour, measurements, and some notes on the habits of the various species, but for a full and scientific history of the subjects, I would refer the reader to *The Mammals of Great Britain and Ireland* by J. G. Millais, *A History of British Mammals* by the late Major Barrett-Hamilton and Martin A. C. Hinton, and Bell's *British Quadrupeds*, 2nd edition, to which I owe much information.

In arranging the classification of the different species, I have followed that of Mr Millais, in his work already mentioned.

AT

HASCOMBE,
GODALMING, *June*, 1920

Mammals Extinct in the British Islands Within Historic Times

THERE ARE FIVE INTERESTING WILD ANIMALS which have become extinct in our islands within historic times, namely, the Wolf, the Brown Bear, the Beaver, the Reindeer, and the Wild Boar.

The Wolf
Canis lupis, Linnaeus

This species was once so numerous as to be a scourge in many parts of the land, and appears to have survived to a later period than any of the others on the list. The many place-names referring to the presence of the animal in widely separated localities show how prevalent it was in past days, and how great an impression it made on the imagination of the people in their homes when the Wolf had literally to be kept from the door, and when places of refuge had to be constructed to shelter travellers among lonely moors and forests.

In England, where it is said to have lingered till about the beginning of the sixteenth century, it had disappeared long before the last were killed in Scotland and Ireland.

In Scotland the great uncleared forests of the Highlands harboured the Wolf until much later, so that it survived there to a comparatively recent date, the last being probably the 'four old ones and some whelps' referred to by Mr Harting (*Extinct British Animals*) as having been killed in Sutherland between 1690 and 1700.

In the Reay country as well as in other parts of Scotland the ravages of the wolves were at one time so terrible as to force the inhabitants to bury their dead on islands such as Handa and others.

In Ireland the Wolf appears to have survived till about 1766 or 1770.

The Brown Bear
Ursos arctos, Linnaeus

The references made by ancient writers relating to the presence of the Bear in Great Britain during the Roman occupation of the country show that it was not uncommon in byegone days when animals from the Caledonian forests were transported to Rome to play their part in the arena.

The Bear appears to have existed in Britain well into Saxon times, but the date of its extinction is uncertain. Later when Bear-baiting became a popular amusement, large numbers of the animals were brought from the Continent of Europe for the purpose.

The Beaver
Castor fiber, Linnaeus

The remains of this species found in various parts of England, Wales and Scotland show that it existed in some numbers, though there is nothing to indicate that it ever inhabited Ireland.

There is some allusion made to this animal in ancient laws, chiefly relating to its valuable fur.

According to Welsh historians, the Beaver was once not uncommon in their rivers, where Pennant says it remained till late in the twelfth century.

The Reindeer
Rangifer tarandus, Linnaeus

The number of horns of the Reindeer found in marl and peat deposits prove the abundance of this species in the British Islands in prehistoric times, and for long afterwards it lingered in Caithness and the Orkneys.

From a passage in the *Orkneyinga Saga*, it appears to have been regularly hunted in the mountains of Caithness by the jarls of Orkney, who in summer crossed to the mainland for this purpose (Harting).

There is a good figure of the animal incised in an ancient monumental stone near Grantown.

The Wild Boar

Sus scrofa, Linnaeus

The Wild Boar was a common beast of the forest inhabiting Britain in early times, and is frequently mentioned in the laws and in books on hunting of those days.

It is said to have been still plentiful in the reign of Henry VIII, though when it actually became extinct in England is uncertain.

Like the Wolf, the Wild Boar has left traces of his presence in the names of many places in the British Islands, showing how common he must have been at one time.

The Roe Deer
[tail-piece from page 49 of the 1920–1 edition]

Plate 1

Order CHEIROPTERA, bats
Family RHINOLOPHIDAE Genus RHINOLOPHUS

The Greater Horse-shoe Bat
Rhinolophus ferrum-equinum, Schreber
pl. 1 **top**

In beginning this short description of our British Bats, it would be well to consider first the chief distinguishing features of these animals, by which the different species may be readily recognised.

There are now known to be twelve distinct species inhabiting the British Islands, whilst a few others formerly on the list are now omitted, two having been wrongly identified, and the others apparently immigrants brought over from the Continent of Europe in vessels.

The form of the ear, with its earlet or tragus placed at the doorway of this organ, the shape of the wings and interfemoral membrane, especially the point of attachment of the former at the ankle or toes, and also the number and character of the teeth, are all useful means of identification.

The Greater and Lesser Horse shoe belong to the group of 'leaf-nosed' Bats, so named on account of the curious nasal appendage surrounding the nostrils, with a lancet-shaped extension over the forehead.

These two species are the only representatives of their kind in the British Islands, though many others showing a wonderful variety in the form of the nose-leaf are found in various parts of the world.

In the Greater Horse-shoe Bat the expanse of wings varies in different individuals, and the females, as in many other species, are larger than the males.

The specimen figured in the Plate obtained in the flesh from Wells, Somersetshire, towards the end of September 1919, measured 12⅜ inches from tip to tip of wings, but examples occur of larger dimensions, even up to 355 millimetres (about 14 inches), according to the late Major Barrett-Hamilton.

The fur, usually brighter in the females, is a warm tawny grey in colour, and paler on the underparts of the animal. A young one received in September, and represented in the lower part of the Plate, was a soft neutral grey in colour.

The ears are sharply pointed with an outward bend at the tips, while a prolongation of their outer margin crosses in front of the auditory opening in a horizontal direction and forms a conspicuous lobe called the antitragus. The tragus, which is such a prominent feature in the ears of the Vespertilionidae or typical Bats, is absent in the Rhinolophidae or Horse-shoe Bats. The remarkable nasal appendage is formed like a horse-shoe in the lower section, from about the centre of this, between the nostrils arises a horn-like protuberance standing out from the face, while above, the frontal leaf narrows to a point over the forehead. Nervous and highly sensitive, it is well supplied with glands, and although its true function is apparently not yet fully understood, it is probably a means of communicating to the Bat an impression of its surroundings, independently of the eyesight. The small and deeply set eyes are more conspicuous than in the Lesser Horse-shoe Bat.

The wings are very broad and arise from the tibia just above the ankle, their wide expanse of membrane no doubt accounting for the ease and buoyancy of flight in this species.

The tail is usually kept in a recurved position over the back and with its membrane does not serve as a pouch when a beetle or other large insect is grappled, as with most other Bats. Mr T. A. Coward, who has devoted much time to the study of these animals, observed that the Greater Horse-shoe on such occasions uses instead the wing membrane as a kind of bag.

The teeth are thirty-two in number.

The Greater Horse-shoe Bat is widely distributed over the temperate parts of Europe, is found also in North Africa, and ranges eastwards to the Himalayas, China, and Japan. In the British Islands it is distinctly a southern species and unknown in Scotland and Ireland.

It appears to be confined chiefly to the southern and southwestern counties in England and to certain parts of Wales.

According to Major Barrett-Hamilton (*A History of British Mammals*, part v. p. 230) the most northerly record for England is Whitchurch, near Ross, Hereford, while more to the eastwards specimens have been taken in Berkshire, and Mr De Winton, as Mr Millais states, has on several occasions seen it hawking for food in the Zoological Gardens of London. It is fairly numerous in Devonshire, Somersetshire, Gloucester and Hampshire, including the Isle of Wight.

Dr Latham was the first to discover the Greater Horse-shoe Bat in England, when he captured one in the powder-mills at Dartford, Kent, an account of which was first published by Pennant in the fourth edition of his *British Zoology* in 1776. Kent's Hole, Torquay, has long been known as a resort of this species, and among other places there is a colony under the roof of Wells Cathedral, whence I obtained the specimen for the Plate.

As a retreat, this Bat loves the darkness and obscurity of natural caverns, underground workings in limestone, or sometimes recesses in old buildings. Describing its flight, Mr Millais says (*Mammals of Great Britain and Ireland*, vol. i. pp. 26–27), 'It hunts for its food – moths and flying beetles, especially the fern-chafer – at an elevation of from thirty to thirty-five feet above the ground. In flight, when seen to advantage, this Bat exhibits more grace than power and activity, the characteristics of the Noctule; it sails and flutters with a delicate butterfly flight which is exceedingly attractive. Its broad wing area is noticeable and gives the animal a larger appearance than it actually possesses. In the open air the flight seems slow but full of grace and buoyancy.'

With regard to its methods of feeding, Barrett-Hamilton states (*A History of British Mammals*, part v. p. 244), 'There can now, I think, be little doubt that the Horse-shoes do not, like most other bats, consume their prey when on the wing, but habitually alight to eat it, conveying it for this purpose to certain favourite dining-places within the shelter of the caves. These, even when the diners are absent, are betrayed by the débris of wings, elytra, and other fragments, as well as by the heaps of excrement which fall to the ground during and after a meal.' The two species of Horse-shoe Bat show a wonderful dexterity in alighting, when in order to perch head downwards they turn a complete somersault.

When hibernating, they hang suspended by their feet, whilst their bodies are almost entirely enshrouded by the wings.

A single young one is born at a time, which is carried by the mother, attached by its teeth to her body. Two have been recorded in Germany.

The Lesser Horse-shoe Bat
Rhinolophus hipposideros, Blanford
pl. 1 **bottom**

Except in size – the expanse of wings measured 8¾ inches in the specimen figured in the Plate – this Bat closely resembles the Greater Horse-shoe, and was first discovered in England and shown to be a distinct species by Montagu, who obtained examples in Wiltshire and later in Kent's Hole, Torquay. Compared with its larger relation, two Lesser Horse-shoe Bats, kindly sent to me by Mr T. A. Coward for illustration in this book, were duller in the colour of the fur, the underparts being of a very pale brownish grey and above a slightly darker shade of the same.

In colour, the young is similar to the immature Greater Horse-shoe.

The nasal ornaments, though resembling those of the larger species, differ in some respects.

The eyes are very small and deeply set, more so than in the other, being almost hidden in the fur. The teeth are the same in number.

The Lesser Horse-shoe Bat inhabits Europe as far north as the Baltic territories, ranging southwards to North and East Africa and eastwards to Kashmir.

In the British Islands it is confined to England, Wales, and Ireland, being common in some parts of the latter country.

The only Scottish record is not now considered reliable.

Though recorded from as far north as Ripon, Yorkshire, it is not till we come to the southern and south-western counties of England and various localities in Wales that it becomes more general, and is often found associating with the Greater Horse-shoe in favourable situations.

continued on page 22

Pl. I.

Plate 2

Family VESPERTILIONIDAE Genus BARBASTELLA

The Barbastelle
Barbastella barbastellus, Schreber
pl. 2 **bottom**

In the opinion of Professor Bell (*British Quadrupeds*), the Barbastelle appears to form a link between the Horse-shoe and the Long-eared Bats. It has only one near ally, namely *B. darjilingensis*, inhabiting the Himalayas.

The wings are fairly broad and measured from tip to tip when expanded $10\frac{1}{8}$ inches in a specimen captured by myself, but larger examples are given by Major Barrett-Hamilton.

The ears, a distinguishing feature in this species, are rather broad and roughly square-shaped, nearly touching each other on their inner margins which arise from the middle of the forehead.

The tragus is large, reaching more than half-way up the ear, and has a protuberance near the base of its outer margin. The lower leg is comparatively long, allowing a large interfemoral membrane, whilst the feet are small.

The fur is soft and fine, conspicuously dark, almost black in colour, but having a hoary appearance especially on the flanks, which are tinged and frosted with grey. The ears, face, and wing membranes are dusky black. Millais mentions a form of a deep red-brown in colour.

The teeth are thirty-four in number.

The Barbastelle is not uncommon in France, where it was first discovered by Daubenton in 1759, and is also found at a considerable height among the Swiss Alps. It ranges from as far north as southern Scandinavia, southwards to North Africa, whilst eastwards its habitat extends far into Asia.

Sowerby first recognised it as a British species from an example obtained early in the nineteenth century at Dartford, Kent.

The Barbastelle is locally distributed, and apparently by no means abundant anywhere in the British Islands, and as far as known is confined to England and Wales. It has often been recorded in the more southern parts of the kingdom, but north of the Wash it appears to be very rare, though two specimens were taken in Cumberland near Carlisle.

Describing its habits Mr Millais writes (*Mammals of Great Britain and Ireland*, vol. i. p. 43): 'Certainly the two specimens which I observed and one of which I shot at Horsham were hawking for food at 9 p.m. in June and July: they flew very low, and with uncertain irregular flight. This Bat can be recognised by this flight – slow and erratic – as well as the exceeding black colour of the pelage; but if in the hand it cannot be confused with any other species, for the ears, springing from the centre of the forehead, are a character which distinguish it from all the other British Bats excepting the long-eared Bat, whose abnormally long ears, however, prevent confusion.'

It was formerly thought to be more or less solitary in disposition and habits, but later information shows that this is not the case, as many instances have occurred showing its gregariousness and sociability. Various situations are chosen as a retreat, including crevices in ruins, under the loose bark of trees, or dark crannies in caves.

I have only once had an opportunity of watching the Barbastelle in life when at Hascombe, Surrey, in July 1902, one flew into my room one night, and after some difficulty, as it showed great dexterity in dodging and twisting, I succeeded in catching it.

The Long-Eared Bat
Plecotus auritus, Linnaeus
pl. 2 **top**

This Bat may be easily identified at any time by the abnormal size of the ears, which measure about $1\frac{1}{2}$ to $1\frac{3}{4}$ inches and are nearly as long as the head and body combined. The tragus is large and very conspicuous when the animal is at rest, as it then points outwards, while the ears are folded backwards as shown in the sketch in the Plate, which was taken from life. The expanse of wings is about 10 inches.

When the little creature is hanging head-downwards and asleep in the daytime or during hibernation, the projecting tragus may easily be mistaken for the ear, as the latter is then entirely hidden and folded beneath the forearm.

The eyes are fuller and more conspicuous than in our other Bats and according to Millais it does not seem to be so sensitive to light as some of the other species.

The feet are large, and the rather long tail projects slightly beyond the membrane. In the adult, the colour of the upper parts is a dull brown, the chest and belly a pale whity-brown, these colours being darker in the young. The teeth are thirty-six in number.

The range of the Long-eared Bat extends over a great part of Europe, and in Asia as far east as China. It also inhabits North Africa. It is found over the greater portion of the British Islands, being common in many localities in England and the Lowlands of Scotland. It is rarer in the Highlands of that country, though it has been found in many places as far north as Sutherland and Inverness-shire.

Mr Millais says it is common about Perth and Dunkeld, and he once obtained one on North Uist, Outer Hebrides.

I have seen one which was picked up in my presence on the railway line at Pitlochry.

It has also been recorded in the Isle of Man, and is abundant in Ireland.

The Long-eared Bat is partial to wooded districts, where it seeks its food of moths and other insects among the foliage and blossoms of trees, often picking them off the leaves.

Dr N. H. Alcock and Mr C. Moffat, writing in the *Irish Naturalist* (December 1901), thus describe its habits, 'To observe this Bat on the wing, it is a good plan to wait at dusk under some tree whose foliage is not too dense to be seen through – an ash is probably the best that can be selected – and watch for its appearance among the branches overhead. From about thirty to thirty-five minutes after sunset, its figure may, almost any summer evening, be thus detected against the sky, gliding and hovering in a stealthy manner among the outer sprays of the tree. It threads its way with a beautiful facility among the twigs and leaves, often seeming rather to swim than to fly, so slight is the visible movement of the wings. Poising at times like a humming bird, it appears to be picking something from the leaves; at other times it suddenly plunges into the middle of a spray, and remains for several seconds clinging to the twigs, no doubt securing or eating insect. It is not uncommon to see one ash tree occupied at the same time by five or six of these Bats – though each comes and departs by itself – all gliding in the same noiseless and lemurine fashion among the leaves, and all to the casual bystander practically invisible. The long ears are often thrown forward so as to resemble a proboscis, and may be distinctly seen if the observer is posted immediately below the Bat.'

From observations made by various naturalists, the Long-eared Bat appears to hunt for prey throughout the whole night, when it can often be recognised by its high-pitched notes.

The specimen shown in the Plate was taken while hibernating under the roof of a neighbour's house where two others were obtained at the same time.

They are also fond of caves as a winter resort, where as far as I have noticed they usually hibernate apart, though other species may inhabit the same cavern.

I have found this so when visiting Mr Heatley Noble's cave near Henley-on-Thames and in another resort used by different species near Godalming. This Bat is easily tamed, and takes more readily to confinement than others.

Pl. 2

Long-eared Bat.
Barbastelle.

$\frac{2}{3}$

Plate 3

Genus VESPERUGO

The Noctule, or Great Bat
Vesperugo noctula, Keyserling and Blasius
pl. 3 **right and bottom**

The Noctule or Great Bat, about the largest of our British species – the Serotine and Greater Horse-shoe alone approaching or equalling it in size – measures in expanse of wings from 13 to 15 inches.

The forehead is broad and low, the muzzle prominent and bulbous, so much so that the eyes are hidden in a full-face view of the head. The nostrils are surrounded by a projecting ridge, the ears set widely apart are broad and rounded, their outer margins extending to below the corner of the mouth. The tragus is short, broad, and rounded at the top. The jaws strong and wide and furnished with powerful teeth, thirty-four in number.

The wings are long, but narrower than the Serotine and have usually a tract of fine golden hair below the forearm.

The tail projects very little beyond the intcrfemoral membrane, and the post-calcarial lobe is large.

The fur, which is very soft and silky in texture, is a fine golden brown in colour, with little difference in the shade of the upper and lower parts. The animal has a disagreeable musky odour.

A specimen obtained in October shortly before hibernating, and figured in the Plate, had become very fat, in preparation for its winter sleep.

The Noctule has a wide distribution over the temperate parts of Europe and Asia, and also inhabits North and East Africa. In England it is more or less common in various localities in the southern, western, and midland counties, and also in Yorkshire, though very rare in Durham and Northumberland. In Wales it is plentiful.

No authentic examples had been obtained in Scotland till October 13th, 1904, when, as recorded by Mr Millais (*Mammals of Great Britain and Ireland*, appendix iii), one was shot at Dalguise, Perthshire, by Mr Charles Eversfield. Another was obtained at Duffus, Elgin, on October 1st, 1909, while some more are said to have been observed near Elgin and Lhanbryde (*Ann. Scott. Nat. Hist.*, 1910, 52–53). There seems to be no authentic record of the occurrence of this species in Ireland.

The Noctule was first detected on the Continent of Europe by Daubenton, and described by him in 1759. Later, in 1771, it was discovered by Gilbert White at Selborne, who obtained two examples in the summer of that year, and gave an accurate description of the animal, which he appropriately named *vespertilis altivolans*, from its manner of feeding high up in the air.

Throughout the year this species is sociable in its habits, large numbers congregating in holes in trees or under the roofs of buildings, the latter being generally used for winter quarters, while in summer, tree-holes are more favoured. Bell, quoting Pennant, states that the Rev Dr Duckhouse saw one hundred and eighty-five taken in one night from the eaves of Queens' College, Cambridge, and Mr Millais, in his *Mammals of Great Britain and Ireland* (vol. i. p. 64), says: 'Near Cambridge and at Frostendon in Suffolk, I have seen large numbers on the wing at the same time. When residing at the latter place in 1883 and 1884 I was much struck with the immense numbers of Noctules which lived in some old oaks in the Rev E. Hickling's grounds; so many as two hundred might be seen on any fine evening in the summer flying above a small meadow only about three acres in size.'

The winter sleep of the Noctule usually lasts from late October until March and early April, though on occasions it has been seen abroad in the months of November, December and February.

The flight of this Bat is swift and powerful, and on fine summer evenings is usually maintained at a high altitude. At other times, probably depending on the state of the weather, the flight is much lower and often quite near the ground or over some sheet of water. Like the Serotine, this species, when pursuing its prey, frequently makes that sudden and characteristic plunge already referred to.

Mr Millais has noted that Noctules often change their hunting-ground, and that a colony may be seen one evening feeding in the immediate neighbourhood of their home-tree, and on another hawking over a meadow more than a mile and a half away.

A great deal has been learned of late years of the habits of this species from the observations of Messrs Coward, Millais, Oldham, Steele, Elliott, and others, which shows that the evening flight only lasts about an hour, when the Bats retire to their dens, emerging again later to continue their hunt till shortly before dawn.

When at rest or in the act of pouching an insect the tail of the Noctule is bent forwards under the body, when in flight it is usually held straight out or curved a little downwards.

The food consists mainly of large flying beetles, which the Bats eat while on the wing, nipping off the strong wing-cases with their powerful teeth.

Mr Oldham, describing the habits of this species (*Zoologist*, 1901, pp. 51–59), says: 'As the light fades, the Bats descend to a lower level, and feed at a height of from fifteen to thirty or forty feet above the fields, pools, and open places in the woods. The crunching of their jaws as they masticate their insect prey may then be heard distinctly.' Wolley describes the cry of the Noctule as a 'cricket-like chirp'.

The Pipistrelle or Common Bat
Pipistrellus pipistrellus, Schreber
pl. 3 **top left**

The expanse of wings in this species averages about 8 inches. The ears are rather oval and comparatively narrower than in the Noctule and Leisler's Bat, the tragus barely half the length of the ear and rounded at the tip. The feet small; teeth thirty-four in number. The colour is usually reddish-brown on the upper parts, a little paler below, but some examples are of a much deeper tint, the darkest I have seen being a dull sooty black.

The Pipistrelle inhabits the temperate parts of Europe, ranging as far as Kashmir in Asia, and also to North Africa.

It is more or less plentiful all over the British Islands, in Scotland occurring as far north as the Orkneys and westwards to the Outer Hebridges. Dr Eagle Clark mentions a pair which he observed at an altitude of 1300 feet at Corrour Lodge, Inverness-shire (*Scottish Naturalist*, December 1917).

It is also plentiful in Ireland.

This species was considered by Pennant, and others who followed him, to be identical with the common Bat of Continental naturalists, namely the mouse-coloured Bat, *Vespertilio murinus*, which is a much larger animal and not now recognized to be British. The Rev L. Jenyns was the first to dispel this confusion and show that our common Bat is the Pipistrelle, which also occurs in Europe.

There are few parts of the country where on fine summer evenings between 'the gloaming and the mirk' this little creature, the smallest of our Bats, may not be seen. With rapid wing-beats it flits along country lanes or threads its way around trees or buildings in search of various small insects, especially gnats, which form its chief food.

Like other Bats, it shows little fear of man, and will circle closely round one's head. The Pipistrelle usually selects some likely beat for the evening hunt, returning to the same spot for many nights in succession.

According to Mr Moffat (*Irish Naturalist*, 1905, pp. 101–103) it appears to hunt for its prey throughout the whole night, retiring to its den shortly before sunrise. It is fond of the neighbourhood of ponds and rivers and drinks like other Bats by sipping the surface of the water as it flies.

The Pipistrelle awakes from its winter sleep earlier than most of its relations, generally appearing on the wing about the middle of March if the weather be fine, and retiring in October or November.

Though this is the general rule, it may be tempted out at almost any time in the winter if a mild spell sets in.

Various situations are chosen as retreats, roofs of cottages, churches, and other buildings, cavities in walls or under the bark of old trees.

In confinement, this species will readily take its food, eating flies or meal worms with avidity, and if any prey be too large to master with its mouth, the tail membrane is used as a pouch.

Pl. 3.

Pipistrelle or Common Bat.

Noctule.

Noctule.

Plate 4

The Serotine
Vesperugo serotinus, Blasius
pl. 4 **left**

This large species, which approaches and sometimes equals the Noctule or Great Bat in size, measures in expanse of wings from about 12 to 14½ inches. The ears are broad with rounded tips, the outer margin terminating in a lobe near the corner of the mouth.

The tragus is larger than in the Noctule and Pipistrelle and ends in a rounded tip. The face, except for a few hairs arising from the glands, is bare.

Compared with the Noctule, the wing is broader, the calcarial lobe very small, and the tip of the tail projects noticeably beyond the interfemoral membrane.

There are thirty-two teeth.

The fur on the back is a rich dark brown in colour and silky in texture, the underparts being paler and greyer.

Of all our Bats, the Serotine appears to have the greatest geographical range, being widely spread over Europe, Asia, Africa and America, and also distinguished in this respect that it is the only species indigenous to both Hemispheres.

In the British Islands it is rare except in a few favoured districts in the southern, and especially the south-eastern, counties of England. Mr Millais, in his *Mammals of Great Britain and Ireland*, mentions Kent as the only county in which it may be said to be common, giving Yalding as a locality where it is numerous, the other places mentioned being Folkestone, Maidstone, Canterbury, Riverschurch, Charlton, Waldershare, Dartford, and Wingham.

It has rarely occurred north of the Thames, two or three having been recorded from Essex; and in the *Zoologist* (1892, p. 403) Mr Coburn mentions a specimen from the neighbourhood of Birmingham.

The Serotine was first described by Daubenton in 1759. Its manner of flight, as described by various observers, appears to differ according to the kind of prey in season, or the state of weather prevailing at the time, as it seems averse to cold and damp. At times it flutters through open spaces sheltered by trees, feeding on cockchafers and other insects, and at others flies high aloft, frequently swooping obliquely downwards in a sudden dive in an effort to secure some insect at a lower level than itself.

The same characteristic dive may also often be noticed in the Noctule.

The late Major Barrett-Hamilton, describing their flight as witnessed at Yalding, says (*A History of British Mammals*, part iii. p. 136):

'They now flew higher, often at thirty or forty feet, but not, I think, exceeding the height of tall elms or of gunshot, and often descending near to the ground. Their flight was not unlike that of the Pipistrelle, but their beat was wider and their pace relatively less rapid. They could not be described as weak fliers, nor was their pace slow, but they clearly lacked the dash and finish of the Noctule, one or two of which were present for comparison.' He also states (p. 137), 'Despite its name, the Serotine is an early flier, perhaps the earliest of all British Bats'.

This species evidently does not fly throughout the whole night, but for how long does not seem to be known precisely. It is sociable in its habits, small parties usually assembling under the roofs of houses or in the hollows of old trees where they retreat during daylight. Hibernation appears to last from October till April.

According to Continental observers a single young one is born at a time.

The Parti-coloured Bat
Vespertilio murinus, Linnaeus
(not shown)

This species was one of those formerly included in the British list, but has now been removed, as the two specimens recorded, one by John Hancock, found on board a ship in Yarmouth Roads, and the other, taken at Plymouth by Dr W. E. Leach, are supposed to have been brought over in vessels from the Continent of Europe.

Leisler's Bat
Vesperugo Leisleri, Keyserling and Blasius
pl. 4 **right**

This species, called by Bell the Hairy-armed Bat, on account of the band of hair extending below the forearm on the under surface of the wing, is intermediate in size between the Pipistrelle and Noctule, and measures about 12 inches in expanse of wings.

In general, the form and character of Leisler's Bat resembles the Noctule's, though less lusty and robust. The feet and legs are comparatively smaller and more slender, and the calcarial lobe also not so large. The teeth are thirty-four in number.

On the upper parts the colour of the fur is a deep brown, the lower greyish brown.

Mr A. Whitaker, who has had exceptionally good opportunities of studying this species alive, thus describes it in *Wild Life* (February 1914, p. 79). 'To my mind, however, the most satisfactory means of distinguishing between these two Bats is afforded by the fur of the Noctule becoming uniformly paler towards the base, while in the species we are considering the reverse is the case, the hairs, especially those of the underparts, being almost black at the roots. By rubbing up the fur of the underparts the wrong way, this distinction is made apparent even in a casual inspection.'

This Bat was first discovered by the German naturalist Leisler and described by Kuhl in 1819.

It inhabits Europe and Asia, where it ranges eastwards to the Himalayas.

In Great Britain, as far as at present known, its range seems very limited.

The late R. F. Tomes, in Bell's *British Quadrupeds* (2nd ed. p. 27), notes 'its not unfrequent appearance at various localities in the course of the river Avon, in the counties of Warwick, Worcester, and Gloucester'. Besides these localities it has been recorded from Cheshire by Mr T. A. Coward (*Zoologist*, 1887, p. 169), whilst in the West Riding of Yorkshire it appears to be plentiful near Barnsley.

In Ireland it is a common Bat in many parts of the country, where it takes the place of the Noctule.

Mr Whitaker, in the article already referred to in *Wild Life* (pp. 79–80), says 'these bats may be seen hawking for food on mild evenings throughout the whole season, spring, summer, and autumn. . . .

'They fly along the low edge of the plantation and often make digressions to a couple of large ash trees growing in an isolated position on the boundary of my garden. Round and round these they will circle with great persistence, snapping up moths, and doubtless other insects also, whenever they flutter out a few feet from the shelter of the foliage. Their flight is stronger and more direct than that of the Pipistrelle, and usually at about twice the altitude; on the other hand it is not quite so high or strong as that of the Noctule.' The earliest and latest dates on which he noticed the Bats abroad were March 3rd and November 9th.

Leisler's Bat is a tree-haunting species, choosing for its den some cavity in the trunk or branches, where it associates with others of its species during the summer months. In winter, when hibernating, it is said to keep apart from its fellows.

From careful observations made by Mr Moffat in Ireland, as quoted by Major Barrett-Hamilton (*A History of British Mammals*), Leisler's Bat does not fly throughout the night, the evening and morning flights lasting a little more than an hour each.

The voice is sharp and high-pitched.

Pl. 4.

Leisler's Bat.

Serotine.

A.Thorburn 1920

Plate 5

Genus MYOTIS

Daubenton's Bat
Myotis Daubentoni, Leisler
pl. 5 **right**

The distinguishing features of this species, by which it may be known at any time from Natterer's Bat, are the shorter ears and tragus, large feet, the projection of the two last tail vertebrae beyond the interfemoral membrane, and the tiny lobe succeeded by a notch on each side of the latter near the tail.

It differs from the Whiskered Bat, not only in the greater size of the feet, but also in the attachment of the wing membrane, which starts from the ankle and not from the base of the outer toe, as in the other.

The expanse of wings in Daubenton's Bat is about 9 inches, occasionally more.

The ears are of medium size with rounded tips, and the tragus, which is straight and pointed, measures about half their length.

The glands are conspicuous on the muzzle, which is fringed with hairs. The teeth number thirty-eight. In colour the upper parts are a glossy umber brown, below pale brownish-grey.

This Bat inhabits Europe and Asia from Scandinavia and Russia to the Mediterranean countries, while eastwards it reaches Japan.

Though known to Leisler and Kuhl on the Continent of Europe, Daubenton's Bat was not fully identified as a British species till Bell described it in the first edition of his *British Quadrupeds* in 1837.

The belief that it was a rare species in the British Islands is now known to be without foundation, as it is common, and probably always has been, in places suited to its water-loving habits.

Gilbert White, writing to Pennant in 1767, mentions having seen some years before that date, 'myriads of bats' between Richmond and Sunbury, and that 'the air swarmed with them all along the Thames'; these masses are most likely to have consisted chiefly of Daubenton's Bats.

Another favourite haunt is Christchurch, Hampshire, where Mr Borrer found it in abundance in 1874, and according to Mr Millais 'it is just as common now'.

The late R. F. Tomes in Bell's *British Quadrupeds* (2nd ed. p. 62) says, 'We have sometimes seen these Bats so thick on the Avon, near to Stratford, that at certain spots there could not have been fewer than one to every square yard'.

It is plentifully distributed throughout the greater part of England and Wales, and is also common in various localities in Scotland, where, according to Dr Eagle Clarke (*Ann. Scott. Nat. Hist.* 1892, p. 266), it has been recorded as far north as Fochabers on the Spey.

It also appears to be widely spread over Ireland.

This species has been aptly called the 'Water Bat', by Major Barrett-Hamilton, who thus describes its habits (*A History of British Mammals*, part iii. p. 149): 'So peculiar are the vespertinal habits of this species, that, although it is locally abundant, an ordinary observer may be quite unconscious of its existence. It is essentially aquatic, if such an expression be applicable to an animal which never enters the water. It haunts that element continually, flying so close to it that it is difficult to distinguish between the creature itself and its reflection.'

I had not come across this Bat in Surrey until this spring (1920), when in February, requiring specimens for the Plate, I made several visits to an artificial cave in the sandstone near Godalming, where I found two hibernating. These were in small crevices among the stones in the roof of the cavern and soon became lively when brought into a warm room. In summer Daubenton's Bat will often use a hollow tree as a retreat during daylight.

From the observations of Mr Moffat (*Irish Naturalist*, 1905, pp. 106–107) it appears to fly throughout the night. Its winter retirement is said to last from the end of September till April.

Natterer's Bat
Myotis Nattereri, Kuhl
pl. 5 **left**

This species, the Reddish-grey Bat of Bell, measuring in expanse of wings 11 inches or sometimes less, is easily distinguished from any other British Bat by the interfemoral membrane, which is furnished along its margin, between the end of the calcar or spur and the tail, with a fringe of stiff hairs not unlike the teeth of a tiny comb. It is also the lightest in colour of all our Bats.

The ears are large and comparatively long; the tragus, which is about two-thirds the length of the ear, is narrow and pointed. There are two prominent glands on each side of the upper part of the muzzle, which is long, naked about the nostrils and lips but fringed with hairs, more or less concealing the eyes. The gape is wide, the point of the lower jaw below the lip furnished with longish hairs. The teeth number thirty-eight. The wings, compared with those of the other members of this genus, are long and broad, the feet small. The fur is soft and long, the colour of the upper parts a pale brown, below greyish white. The bases of the hairs above and below are very dark.

This species is found throughout the greater part of Europe, and according to Barrett-Hamilton, ranges in Asia to Japan, where it is represented by a sub-species.

In England and Wales, there are few counties where it has not occurred, being common in some localities. Across the border in Scotland it is hardly known, the only reliable evidence of its occurrence there is a specimen in the British Museum from Inveraray, Argyll, while a skin in the collection of the late Robert Grey were supposed to be from Midlothian.

There are various records for Ireland.

Natterer's Bat is fond of well-watered woodland country and is sociable in its habits.

The late R. F. Tomes, writing in Bell's *British Quadrupeds* (2nd ed. pp. 55–56) describes a colony found under the church roof at Arrow, near Alcestor; here the Bats were clustered in a mass three or four inches thick, six or seven wide and about four feet in length, while a constant movement was going on, as those on the outside endeavoured to push their way inwards, probably for warmth.

As a winter retreat, Natterer's Bat shows a partiality for caves. Mr Heatley Noble tells me it is common near Henley-on-Thames, where it hibernates in a cave in the chalk.

Near Godalming, Surrey, in the cavern already referred to in the account of Daubenton's Bat, I have found it on several occasions hibernating in the vaulted roof. They were all separately lodged in deep crevices among the stones, and sometimes entirely hidden from sight. When disturbed, they uttered a peevish chattering squeak. Two of these, which I kept in confinement for a few days, were very gentle in their habits and usually slept in their cage closely touching each other in the darkest corner they could find.

They became very vigorous when wakened by the warmth of a room and if let out would fly for a considerable time, showing a marvellous skill in turning and twisting as they searched every corner in the hope of finding an outlet. The tail, as far as I could discover, was usually held straight out, but occasionally would be slightly curved downwards. They showed no fear as they circled at times round my head, at others quite low down by my feet. Although they would sometimes attempt to bite when handled, their delicate teeth did not appear to be capable of penetrating the skin.

Natterer's Bat is fond of hawking for its food over pools of water like Daubenton's Bat, but, according to Mr Millais, it feeds at a greater elevation than the other. It appears to prey on gnats and similar insects, but the only food I could persuade my captives to take was milk.

Pl. 5.

Daubenton's Bat.

Natterer's Bat.

Plate 6

Whiskered Bat
Myotis mystacinus, Leisler
pl. 6 **left**

The Whiskered Bat, scarcely larger than the Pipistrelle, measures in expanse of wings 8½ inches. The short and rather stumpy face and muzzle, nearly black in the colour of the naked parts, are bushy with the numerous fine hairs which conceal the eyes, while the hairy fringe on the upper lip accounts for the name of this species.

The dusky black ears are rounded at the tips and notched on their outer margin. The tragus, measuring fully half the length of the ear, ends in a blunt point. The wings arise from the base of the outer toes, while the tail projects slightly beyond the membrane. The teeth are thirty-eight in number.

The colour of the hair tips on the upper parts of the body is a pale brown, on the under parts dull grey, the bases of the hairs above and below a dusky black. I am indebted to Mr T. A. Coward for the specimen figured in the plate, which was taken while hibernating early in February. This Bat was extremely dark in colour and a typical example of the species in its winter coat.

The Whiskered Bat is widely distributed over the Continent of Europe, from as far north as Scandinavia and Russia southwards to France and Spain. In Asia, it reaches China, Sikkim and Nepaul, and also occurs in North Africa.

In the British Islands the Whiskered Bat was formerly considered rare, but this belief was no doubt owing to the lack of observation and the difficulty of distinguishing this small species when on the wing from the Pipistrelle or Common Bat.

More recently the alertness of various naturalists has shown that it is plentiful in some localities.

In England it is numerous in various parts of the southern, western and midland counties, and also in Yorkshire, though rare or absent in East Anglia, Durham and Northumberland. In Wales it is uncommon.

There are only two records of its capture in Scotland, namely, one near Rannoch, Perthshire, in June 1874, and another at Dunbar, East Lothian, 20th March, 1893. It is widely distributed in Ireland.

The habits of the Whiskered Bat seem to have been less closely watched than those of most of the other species inhabiting our islands. It has been supposed to be less sociable in its manners than others, though R. F. Tomes (*Vict. Hist.*, '*Worcester*') mentions a colony of more than a hundred in the roof of his house at Littleton. It often frequents the neighbourhood of rivers, where it has been observed seeking its prey among the branches of trees or flitting over the surface of the water, while it is said to have been more often noticed hawking during daylight than other species.

Bechstein's Bat
Myotis Bechsteini, Leisler
pl. 6 **right**

This rare species, though resembling Natterer's Bat in colour, may always be known by the much larger ears, the comparatively shorter tragus and the absence of the fringe of short bristles on the interfemoral membrane.

The wings, arising from the base of the toes, measure about 11 inches from tip to tip when expanded. Mr Millais, who was fortunate enough to capture one alive in Mr Heatley Noble's cave near Henley-on-Thames on March 1, 1901, says (*Mammals of Great Britain and Ireland*, vol. i. pp. 97–98): 'It is reddish brown above, the hair being parti-coloured, lighter at the tips and pale grey beneath, though not quite so light as in *M. Nattereri*. By far the most striking feature, and one which even a casual observer may note, is the size and shape of the ears. They first bend outwards at an angle of 78°, and then turn upwards to the perpendicular, ending in a rounded point.'

The teeth are thirty-eight in number. As far as is known, this species is confined to Europe, where it ranges from Scandinavia to Italy and Spain. It has only rarely been taken in England and was first recorded in the New Forest, where Millard obtained a specimen, now preserved in the British Museum, more than eighty years ago. Again in the New Forest, Mr E. W. A. Blagg found a party of fully a dozen in a Woodpecker's hole in July 1886. Of these he kept two and later gave them to the British Museum. The next recorded was one shot by Mr W. C. Ruskin Butterfield near Battle, Hastings, on July 28th, 1896. Next comes Mr Millais' specimen from Henley-on-Thames and two more were obtained by Mr Percy Wadham near Newport, Isle of Wight, on July 31st and August 14th, 1909. This completes the list of those captured in the British Islands, as far as I know.

Little appears to be known of the habits of this fine bat. In Germany it is said to inhabit holes in trees and to hibernate under the roofs of houses. Its flight, beginning late in the evening, is stated to be slow and at a low elevation.

Mr Millais' specimen was discovered in a crevice in the chalk of the cave, in which were found at the same time several other species. I am indebted to him for kindly lending me a photograph of this example, taken shortly after death, from which I have been able in the Plate to show the correct form of the ears.

---

continued from Plate 1

The Lesser Horse-shoe Bat

Though found locally in some numbers, it can scarcely be called a common species, though it has a much wider distribution than its cousin.

Among other haunts, according to Millais, it frequents Kensington Gardens in London, and owing to the difficulty in identifying the different species, when hawking after their prey in the dusk of evening, this Bat may possibly be less rare than one might be led to suppose.

This frail little creature, which is said to be more delicate than any other European Bat, seldom venturing out unless in calm weather, is difficult to keep in confinement for more than a few days.

To Mr T. A. Coward and Mr C. Oldham we owe most of our knowledge of its ways and habits in this country.

In *The Mammals of Great Britain and Ireland*, pp. 36–37, Mr Millais quotes the following account supplied to him by Mr Coward, 'In every case the Bats were hanging: some were suspended from a smooth roof, clinging to minute inequalities, others were at the top of holes in the caves; in such positions the face of the Bat was always turned towards the nearest wall. Both sexes hung in company; the largest gathering consisted of ten Bats. In one water-worn hole a male and female were together, an inch or two apart. When first found the Bats all hung with perfectly straight legs; their ears were partly folded back, and their faces hidden. They noticed the light at once, and began to sway slowly from side to side; then they bent their long legs and drew themselves up, swinging with more vigour. The tail in every case was recurved over the back. . . .

'When alighting after a short flight the agility of the Bat was most noticeable. Most Bats when they alight seize the object on which they are settling with the thumbs, and then rapidly turn round and take hold with the feet. The Horse-shoes, when an inch or so from the object, turn in the air, taking hold at once with the feet.'

Like the Greater Horse-shoe Bat, it usually chooses as a retreat dark caverns of limestone formation, or recesses in old buildings, hanging with its body almost wholly draped with the wings. Various observers have noticed the marvellous skill with which this species avoids any obstacle during flight.

In Bell's *British Quadrupeds*, 2nd ed. pp. 98–99, the late R. F. Tomes, describing its powers, says 'It literally flew into every part of the room, and behind and under everything, even under a bookcase standing against a wall, although there was scarcely a space of three inches between it and the floor. Some bookshelves in a recess especially attracted its attention, and after examining them diligently, it flew into a vacancy occasioned by the removal of a moderate octavo volume, and again into the open room, without having so much as touched anything with the tips of its wings.'

Pl. 6.

Bechstein's Bat. $\frac{2}{3}$

Whiskered Bat.

Plate 7

Order INSECTIVORA, insect-eating mammals
Family ERINACEIDAE Genus ERINACEUS

The Hedgehog
Erinaceus europaeus, Linnaeus
pl. 7

The list of the British Insectivora or insect-eating mammals is comparatively short, namely the Hedgehog, the Mole, and three species of Shrews. The Hedgehog or Urchin, whose length from nose to root of tail varies from about 8 to 10 inches, is common in many country districts. The armour of strong prickly spines covering the greater part of the body is so controlled by muscular action that when required the sharp points can project in almost every direction, while the head and other vulnerable parts may be quickly withdrawn under their protection. The spines, yellowish white in colour, with a dark band towards the points, are closely set in the tough skin, and under normal conditions, as when the animal is in movement, they follow the line of the body and lie pointing backwards.

A covering of stiff pale-brown or whitish hairs clothes the other parts of the body. The snout and face are dark, especially round the eyes.

The spiny coat affords such effective protection when the animal is tightly curled into a ball that few enemies care to tackle it, though a high-couraged terrier, in spite of severe punishment, will force an entrance, while the Fox and Badger are also able to overcome it. It is not known how the two latter animals manage to do this. Mr Millais considers (*Mammals of Great Britain and Ireland*) that they may employ the same method as a dog he once met with, which, in attacking, worked with the nails of the forepaws until he got one of the latter fixed against the chest of his quarry 'while with the other he drew up the head and forced it back. Then he gave one nip and the tragedy was over.'

The cries of a Hedgehog when attacked by a Badger are said to be pitiful (*Field*, March 23rd, 1875).

Referring to the strength and elasticity of the Hedgehog's armour, Bell in his *British Quadrupeds* (1st ed. p. 77) says, 'I have repeatedly seen a domesticated Hedgehog in my possession run toward the precipitous wall of an area and without hesitation, without a moment's pause of preparation, throw itself off, and contracting at the same instant into a ball, in which condition it reached the ground from a height of twelve or fourteen feet: after a few moments it would unfold itself and run off unhurt.' I have noticed similar tactics while sketching one of these animals placed on a table, when it would often throw itself over in order to reach the floor.

The shortness of the legs causes a characteristic creeping action in the movements of the Hedgehog, as he makes his way hither and thither in a somewhat stealthy manner after the beetles and other insects which form the chief part of his food.

This animal is widely distributed over Europe from Scandinavia and Russia to the Mediterranean Countries, and in Asia reaches eastwards as far as China.

It is plentiful throughout the greater part of the British Islands, and though scarce in the Northern Highlands of Scotland has been recorded by Dr Eagle Clarke at an altitude of 1400 feet in Inverness-shire (*Scottish Naturalist*, December 1917). It is common in Ireland.

The Hedgehog is more or less nocturnal in its habits, though often coming out to feed in the open air about sundown and occasionally earlier in the day. It takes little notice of human beings unless closely approached or touched, when, trusting to its strong defensive covering, it makes no effort to escape.

Its food is very varied, consisting of insects of different sorts – grasshoppers I have found to be peculiarly attractive – worms, small mammals, and young birds.

It is also said to prey on the viper and common snake and to possess immunity from snake-poison.

The Hedgehog usually retreats for hibernation about the end of November or beginning of December, though it may appear again at intervals during the winter.

One I found asleep on December 24th, 1918, was beneath a bramble bush in a copse, where in a slight hollow in the ground it had prepared a bed of leaves and grass which entirely covered the animal.

It seemed to resent disturbance, as on visiting the place some days later I found the occupant had gone.

The Hedgehog usually breeds twice in the year, about four or five young being born at a time. Gilbert White observed that they are quite white at first, possess little hanging ears, and can in part draw their skin down over their faces, though unable to contract themselves into a ball.

Pl. 7.

Hedgehog.

Plate 8

Family TALPIDAE Genus TALPA

The Common Mole
Talpa europaea, Linnaeus
pl. 8

Living an almost entirely underground life, the form of the Mole is wonderfully adapted for this kind of existence, the elongated flexible snout, cylindrical body, and great muscular power of the forearm and hand enabling it to make its subterranean galleries with great ease and speed.

The hands or forefeet, armed with strong claws, usually turn outwards from the body, but can when required bend downwards with their palms towards the ground if used to hold a worm. The hind feet, compared with the hands, are small and weak. The eyes, extremely minute, are hidden by the surrounding fur, and the question whether they are used by the animal has been often raised. Yet the Mole when above ground seems to have some glimmering of sight. One I kept alive for a day or two when making sketches for the Plate would sometimes slightly raise its head, at the same time partly opening out the fur concealing the eyes, these appeared as tiny black dots on the naked skin.

No external part of the ear is visible.

The tail, measuring slightly more than an inch in length and clothed with bristly hairs, is cocked upwards when the animal is excited. The soft and velvety coat is wonderfully adapted to prevent any soil from lodging in the fur, which arises perpendicularly from the body and can bend either backwards or forwards, according to the movements of the animal in its tunnel.

The colour is a soft deep black with a silvery sheen, the underpart of the chin and belly suffused with a yellowish tinge.

Our Common Mole inhabits Europe from Sweden and Russia to the central parts of France, while south of the Alps and in the Mediterranean countries its place is taken by a closely allied form.

Throughout England, Wales and Scotland it is abundant in suitable localities, and in the latter country has been recorded in the hilly districts at an altitude of over 2000 feet as well as among the sandhills by the sea. I have observed it on the surface of the ground routing amongst gravel and heather by a stream high up on a Highland deer-forest, while there are few places provided with a good supply of earthworms where the Mole may not be found, as these supply its favourite food. The larvae of insects, small mammals, reptiles, and even the flesh of its own kind are also eaten.

It is absent in many of the Scottish islands, including the Shetlands, Orkneys, and Outer Hebrides, and also in the Isle of Man and Ireland.

Most people are familiar with the little earth-mounds which are raised by the Mole when removing the earth from the tunnels as it burrows in search of its prey.

The first systematic study of these runs and the fortress or breeding stronghold was made by the Frenchman, Henri le Court, towards the end of the eighteenth century, and since then many other observers, especially Mr Lionel Adams and Mr W. Evans, have added much to our knowledge. From the fortress a main underground thoroughfare passes through the territory occupied by the Moles, whence branch many byways used when hunting for worms. The ground occupied by the female is said to possess no chief highways, having only runs branching in various directions. Within the breeding stronghold or nursery is placed the nest of leaves and grass in which the young are born, in April or May. These are four or five in number, but may be more or less.

The Mole leads an active strenuous life, with short intervals for repose, and being usually hungry eats enormous quantities of food. One I kept in confinement for a short time consumed large numbers of worms, and was so keen and ravenous that it would allow me to stroke its fur while feeding. After a meal it would rest for a time, apparently asleep. It seemed very sensitive to any sudden noise, and visibly started if I made a slight squeaking note with the lips.

During a hot and dry spell of weather in summer Moles may often be seen above ground.

Pl. 8.

A.Thorburn
1918

Mole.   ⅔

Plate 9

Family SORICIDAE Genus SOREX

The Common Shrew
Sorex araneus, Linnaeus
pl. 9 **top left**

The insectivorous habits, long pointed snout, diminutive eyes, and short velvety fur, show that the Shrews are allied to the Mole and not to the mice, to which they have superficial resemblance.

Our Common Shrew measures in length of head and body just under 3 inches. The tail (about 1½ inches) is proportionately much shorter than that of the Lesser Shrew. The teeth, unlike those of the White-toothed Shrew of France and Germany, are of a reddish-brown colour towards their points. The animal has a strong musky odour.

The colour of the fur on the upper parts varies a good deal in intensity, from a pale brown or rusty brown in summer to a much darker tint in winter. The underparts are dull greyish or yellowish white.

The Common Shrew is widely distributed, ranging throughout a great part of Europe and in Norway, according to Collett, is found as high up as the snow line. It also inhabits the northern parts of Asia and America.

This species is common in suitable localities over the whole of England and Wales, as well as the mainland of Scotland, though unknown in the Shetlands, Orkneys and Outer Hebrides, and also in Ireland. In the three last mentioned localities where it is absent, its place is taken by the Lesser Shrew.

Though the Common Shrew is often about during the winter months, it is in spring, summer, and autumn that it is most frequently seen as it dodges out and in among the grass and dead leaves on hedgerow banks or in gardens and meadows.

During the breeding season in spring, the males often engage in battle. A combat of this kind is described by Mr Millais, who observed two which were contending so fiercely that they fell headlong down a bank while locked in a deadly embrace. The food consists chiefly of slugs, worms, and the larvae of insects, of which it consumes large quantities.

What has long been a puzzle to naturalists is the cause of the strange mortality among Shrews, occurring chiefly in the autumn, when numbers are found lying dead by wayside paths. Various reasons have been suggested as the cause, but the mystery is still unsolved.

In olden days this species was for long the victim of superstition and prejudice, various evils and misfortunes having been attributed to it, such as the lameness of cattle as a result of the passing of a Shrew over their feet or legs.

The well known description by Gilbert White of how these evils were believed to be curable by means of a Shrew-Ash may be quoted here. 'Now a shrew-ash is an ash whose twigs or branches, when gently applied to the limbs of cattle, will immediately relieve the pains which a beast suffers from the running of a shrew-mouse over the part affected: for it is supposed that a shrew-mouse is of so baneful and deleterious a nature, that wherever it creeps over a beast, be it horse, cow, or sheep, the suffering animal is afflicted with cruel anguish and threatened with the loss of the use of the limb. Against this accident, to which they were continually liable, our provident forefathers always kept a shrew-ash at hand, which when once medicated, would maintain its virtue for ever. A shrew-ash was made thus: – Into the body of the tree a deep hole was bored with an augur, and a poor devoted shrew-mouse was thrust in alive, and plugged in, no doubt with several quaint incantations long since forgotten.'

According to Bell, from five to seven young ones are born at a time about the middle of April. These are reared in a nest of grass or dead leaves in a hollow of the ground protected by herbage or similar cover. On the other hand I have seen a nest, consisting of dead oak leaves and containing young as late as November 19th. This was found in a collection of old faggots in my garden.

The Lesser or Pigmy Shrew
Sorex minutus, Linnaeus
pl. 9 **top right**

To the Rev L. Jenyns is due the credit of having first pointed out that the Lesser Shrew differed from the larger species, describing it under the name of *Sorex rusticus*.

This tiny creature, the least of our British Mammals, measures barely 2 inches from snout to root of tail, the length of the tail, without the terminal hairs, being about 1½ inches. Apart from the smaller and more delicately formed body and feet and more elongated snout, the long thickly haired tail is a sure means of distinguishing this species from the Common Shrew.

The colour of the upper parts is a pale brown, paler I think than in the larger species, and in the living specimen which served as a model for the figure in the Plate, the soft velvety fur of the body had a beautiful silvery gloss. The underparts are dull white.

The Lesser Shrew ranges from the British Islands through the greater part of Europe and over northern Asia, where it has been found within the Arctic circle (Dobson). Eastwards it reaches the Pacific, while closely allied forms represent it in America.

In the British Islands it is probably much more plentiful than would appear from the casual notices of its appearance, as its presence in any locality may easily pass unnoticed.

In the neighbourhood of Hascombe, Surrey, I have come across it as often, perhaps more often, than the Common Shrew, but in general it seems to be more sparsely distributed in England than the other.

The Lesser Shrew is common in many parts of Scotland and has even been recorded from the top of Ben Nevis, where a cat at the observatory brought home a specimen.

It is known on many of the Western Islands, being plentiful in the Outer Hebrides and has been recorded in the Orkneys, but not in the Shetlands. This Shrew is abundant in Ireland where it is the only species.

In habits it resembles the Common Shrew, inhabiting hedgerow banks and meadows. It is apparently active in the winter, as I have more than once caught it in traps set to catch mice in an apple loft under the roof of my house.

Though hardy as regards severe cold under natural conditions the constitution of this little animal is yet extremely frail and sensitive to any kind of shock or untoward circumstances, even a few minutes' detention in a trap being fatal, according to information supplied to Barrett-Hamilton by Mr A. H. Cocks (*A History of British Mammals*, part ix. p. 121).

Its hold on life is so slight that it soon dies in confinement, even when caught by hand and uninjured.

One brought to me by a man working in my garden at first appeared quite lively and readily took the flies I provided while making the sketches for the figure in the Plate, but soon a gradual change began and it was dead in a few hours.

When feeding the long flexible snout was bent in almost any direction, while the fore feet were not used to hold the flies when eating, entirely different from the action of a mouse in similar circumstances.

At times the Lesser Shrew seems quite indifferent to the presence of human beings. I once observed one among some grass on a lawn which allowed me to approach so closely and seemed so tame that I caught some flies which it at once devoured, and becoming still more familiar it moved on to the palm of my hand and allowed me to lift it from the ground.

This is the only instance I have met with of such unusual tameness in a wild animal, but Mr Millais mentions a somewhat similar case when a Water Vole allowed itself to be stroked (*Mammals of Great Britain and Ireland*, appendix). The nest and number of young are much the same as those of the Common Shrew.

28

continued on page 30

Pl. 9.

Common Shrew.

Water Shrew.

Lesser Shrew

$\frac{3}{4}$

continued from Plate 9

Genus NEOMYS

The Water Shrew
Neomys fodiens, Pallas
pl. 9 **bottom**

This beautiful species is the largest of our Shrews, measuring in length of head and body from about 3 to 3½ inches, with a tail measurement of about 2 inches.

The colour of the upper parts is usually a deep black with a slaty gloss, while the underparts are normally white, though sometimes darker, with a rusty tinge. The orifice of the ear is 'feathered' with white hairs, and also the under surface of the tail. A darker form of this species often occurs with the whole body above and below more or less dusky, which was at one time considered distinct, and described and figured by Bell as the Oared Shrew (*Sorex remifer*).

Like the other British species, the Water Shrew has its teeth tipped with rust colour.

The form of this animal is well adapted to its aquatic habits, the toes as well as the tail being fringed with hairs which are of use when swimming and diving. Compared with its allies the snout of the Water Shrew is thicker and more powerful.

The Water Shrew has a wide range in Europe, from as far north as Russia to Spain and Italy, while eastwards in Asia it reaches the Altai Mountains. In Great Britain it is well distributed over England, Wales, and the mainland of Scotland, but unknown in Ireland.

As its name implies, the Water Shrew favours the neighbourhood of streams, where it is usually found about the margins of the quieter and more sluggish waters, or seen swimming in their clear pools. It is not however afraid of rapid waters, for I have seen it in quite a swift running stream in Norway, as it swam with its body silvered with air bubbles just under the surface.

The following account of its habits has been given by J. F. M. Dovaston in *Loudon's Mag., Nat. Hist.* ii. 219: 'It dived and swam with great agility and freedom, repeatedly gliding from the bank under water, and disappearing under the mass of leaves at the bottom, doubtless in search of its insect food. It very shortly returned and entered the bank, occasionally putting its long sharp nose out of the water, and paddling close to the edge. This it repeated at frequent intervals from place to place, seldom going more than two yards from the side, and always returning in about half a minute. Sometimes it would run a little on the surface, and sometimes timidly and hastily come ashore, but with the greatest caution, and instantly plunge in again.'

The prey of the Water Shrew is very various, consisting of aquatic insects and their larvae, worms, molluscs, frogs and small fishes, while sometimes the flesh of dead mammals is eaten.

The young, which are said to vary in number from five to eight, are provided with a nest of moss and herbage, placed under the surface of the ground.

Plate 10

Order CARNIVORA, flesh-eating mammals
Family FELIDAE Genus FELIS

The Wild Cat
Felis catus, Linnaeus
pl. 10

Fierce and bloodthirsty in disposition and possessed of great strength and activity, this typical beast of prey is perfectly adapted by nature for a life of rapine.

The male, as a rule larger than the female, measures in length of head and body about 2 feet, with the addition of another 12 or 14 inches as the length of the tail. Millais mentions an exceptionally fine specimen killed at Kinloch Moidart, Ross-shire, in October 1899, which measured 3 feet 10 inches from the nose to the tip of tail.

Compared with the domestic cat, which it often resembles in colour and markings, the true Wild Cat is much more muscular and robust, and possesses a bushy unpointed tail.

The ground colour of the long thick fur of the Wild Cat is in general a tawny or russet grey, beautifully banded and marked with black, the tail barred with the same colour, and the soles of the feet also black. Parts of the chest and belly usually white. The markings on the female are said to be less distinct.

This species inhabits wild wooded districts in most of the European countries.

In England it has long been extinct, and the same may be said of Wales, but in the more remote deer forests of the Highlands of Scotland it still exists, chiefly in Argyllshire, the north-western parts of Inverness-shire, Ross-shire, and the Reay Forest, Sutherland.

The Wild Cat still holds its own or did quite recently in the wilds of Knoydart on the west coast, where it has a typical fastness in the forest sanctuary, a rough rocky hill clothed with birches and old rowans, whence in the winter months it sallies forth to prey on rabbits or game in the home plantations. The true Wild Cat has never inhabited Ireland.

Mr Millais, in his *Mammals of Great Britain and Ireland* (vol. i. p. 176) has graphically described its methods of attack as follows: 'Emerging at dawn and before sunset, this stealthy animal creeps in and out of the forest growth and rocks looking for its prey. When the victim is discovered it is carefully stalked by sight alone until closely approached, when the Cat rushes in with a series of immense forward bounds. So swift is this final attack that four-footed game finds it impossible to escape, even if its terror-paralysed nerves did not benumb its muscles.'

Charles St John, who was well acquainted with this animal, says (*Wild Sports and Natural History of the Highlands*, 8th ed. pp. 44–45): 'Inhabiting the most lonely and inaccessible ranges of rock and mountain, the wild cat is seldom seen during the daytime; at night (like its domestic relative) he prowls far and wide, walking with the same deliberate step, making the same regular and even track, and hunting its game in the same tiger-like manner; and yet the difference in the two animals is perfectly clear. . . . In the hanging birchwoods that border some of the Highland streams and lochs, the wild cat is still not uncommon, and I have heard their wild and unearthly cry echo far in the quiet night as they answer and call to each other.'

According to Millais two to five young are born at a time, usually in May.

Pl. 10

Wild Cat. ♂

Plate 11

Genus VULPES

The Fox
Canis vulpes, Linnaeus
pl. 11

The Fox varies considerably in size, from the Lowland race measuring in length of head and body about 2 feet 3 inches with a tail of about 1 foot, to the much larger animal inhabiting the hills of Scotland, which may measure in total length from nose to tip of tail as much as 5 feet or more, and is also greyer in colour. This is in general a combination of reddish tawny-grey and rust colour on the upper parts, and white, or sometimes dusky-grey below. Upper surface of the ears black towards the tips, with longish white hairs inside the orifice. The feet black above, brown underneath. The white tip to the tail or brush is said to be more conspicuous in the dog Fox than in the Vixen, but individuals of both sexes are occasionally without it. The strong unpleasant odour of the Fox is caused by a fetid secretion in the sub-caudal gland, this 'foxey' effluvium being intensified when the animal is excited.

Foxes, the same or only slightly differing in colour from our British race, are found throughout Europe, while other species inhabit Asia, Africa, and North America, those in the latter country being very closely related to our Common Fox.

The latter is plentiful all over the mainland of Great Britain and Ireland. It is by far the most intelligent and cunning of all our beasts of chase, and endless tales have been told of the wiles and subterfuges employed to escape its enemies or circumvent its prey, from the days of Aesop to our own times. Except in the breeding season the Fox is unsocial and lives apart from his kind, usually occupying an earth or burrow made by some other animal, those dug by the Badger being often taken possession of, or even shared with the owner.

Foxes pair in the winter months, when the weird harsh cry of the vixen may often be heard at night as she calls to her mate, while the latter reveals his presence by two or three sharp little barks. The cubs, up to seven in number, are born about the end of March, and when old enough will come out to play and scamper around the entrance of their home, when their antics are most entertaining to watch.

As is often the case, I was told that the vixen never interfered with some fowls living close at hand, but would always forage for food at a distance. She was no doubt wise enough to know that her young might be endangered if depredations occurred near home.

Various are the ruses employed by the Fox when hunting his prey. Charles St John, in *Natural History and Sport in the Highlands* (8th ed. pp. 195–196), describes how at daybreak he once watched one planning an attack on some hares feeding in the open, first preparing an ambush by scraping a hollow in the ground where he knew by instinct his quarry would pass when leaving the field after sunrise. As soon as a hare came sufficiently near his post, Reynard by a sudden rush seized and killed her immediately.

At times the Fox employs entirely different tactics, and will apparently make use of the curiosity or liability to fascination in the nature of any bird or other animal he may wish to circumvent.

As an instance of this, while walking some years ago along a Hampshire lane in June, my attention was attracted by the unusual crowing of a cock Pheasant among some tall grass in a meadow on the other side of the hedge. On making my way through a gap I saw a Fox some thirty yards away from the bird, circling around his prey yet without appearing to notice it. The Pheasant, although quite aware of his enemy's presence, was making no attempt to escape, and I think the Fox was trying to approach near enough for a sudden spring, when they both saw me and each made off.

Pl. II.

Plate 12

Sub-Order PINNIPEDIA, walrus and seals
Family TRICHECHIDAE Genus TRICHECHUS

The Walrus
Trichechus rosmarus, Linnaeus
pl. 12

The Walrus or Morse – the first-mentioned name being derived from the Scandinavian Hvalros ('Whale-horse'), the latter from the Russian Morss ('Sea-horse') – inhabits the Polar seas and has only rarely been seen or captured in British waters.

The adult Walrus usually measures about 10 or 11 feet in length, but old males often exceed this and will even reach 15 feet in length.

This animal is remarkable for the great bulk and weight of its body and corresponding strength, and will weigh up to 3000 pounds. (Millais).

The long curved tusks, possessed by both sexes, are used as weapons of defence, and are also necessary to the animal when grubbing up molluscs among rocks and shingle while feeding under water. They are also said by some authors to be a help in climbing ice or rocks. The muzzle is furnished with a thick moustache of bristles, the skin on the face is wrinkled with seams and furrows and on the shoulders forms massive folds.

The colour of the Walrus is in general a pale yellowish brown, becoming deeper and redder on the underparts, but the hair on the older animals often wears away or disappears, leaving bare the leathery surface of the skin.

This animal inhabits the northern circumpolar seas of both the Old and New Worlds, but is now much more restricted in its range than formerly. In North America it is still occasionally found as far south as the coast of Labrador, where once it was numerous, while in Europe it reaches the coast of Finmark.

Large herds used to frequent the seas around Spitzbergen, which are now deserted or where they only appear in small numbers. Though mentioned long ago as a visitor to the Scottish coast, the first reliable record was of one killed in the Outer Hebrides at Caolas Stocknis, Harris, in December 1817. This specimen, measuring some 10 feet in length, was seen and described by MacGillivray.

According to Dr Edmonston one was killed in the Shetlands in 1815, and another was obtained on Edday, Orkneys, in June 1825, while the last appears to have been killed by Capt. MacDonald, R.N., on the East Haskeir, near Harris, in April 1841. There is also good evidence showing that others have been seen at various times in British waters.

The Walrus makes his home among the ice-flows surrounding the frozen lands of the far north, where they herd in large colonies and pass their time, when not in the water, in sleeping or sunning themselves on the ice.

Dr Kane, in his *Arctic Explorations* (pp. 243–246), thus describes the animal and its habits: 'The specimens in the museums of collectors are imperfect, on account of the drying of the skin of the face against the skull. The head of the Walrus has not the characteristic oval of the seal; on the contrary, the frontal bone is so covered as to present a steep descent to the eyes and a square, blocked-out aspect to the upper face. The muzzle is less protruding than the seal's, and the cheeks and lips are completely masked by the heavy quill-like bristles.

'Add to this the tusks as a garniture to the lower face, and you have for the Walrus a grim ferocious aspect peculiarly his own. I have seen him with tusks nearly 30 inches long; his body not less than 18 feet. When of this size he certainly reminds you of the elephant more than any other living creature. . . . The instinct of attack which characterises the Walrus is interesting to the naturalist, as it is characteristic also of the land animals, the pachyderms, with which he is classed. When wounded he rises high out of the water, plunges heavily against the ice, and strives to raise himself with his fore-flippers upon its surface. As it breaks under his weight, his countenance assumes a still more vindictive expression, his bark changes to a roar, and the foam pours out of his jaws till it froths his beard. Even when not excited he manages his tusks bravely. They are so strong that he uses them to grapple the rocks with, and climbs steeps of ice and land which would be inaccessible to him without their aid. He ascends in this way rocky islands that are sixty and a hundred feet above the level of the sea; and I have myself seen him in these elevated positions basking with his young in the cool sunshine of August and September.'

The same author describes their voice as 'something between the mooing of a cow and the deepest baying of a mastiff, very round and full, with its bark or detached notes repeated rather quickly seven or nine times in succession.'

Around the breathing holes, which are made among much thicker ice than those of the seals, he observed numbers of broken clam-shells, and, in one instance some gravel, mingled with about half a peck of the coarse shingle of the beach.

The natural increase of this species is slow, as only a single young one is born at a time, which according to Bell is suckled by the mother for nearly two years, so that a period of three or four seasons ensues between birth of the calves. By the time they are weaned their tusks have grown several inches in length, enabling them to forage for themselves.

ADDITIONAL NOTE

As exception has been taken to the inclusion of this species as a British Mammal, it may be interesting to note that Mr Henry Jamieson, Keeper of the Skerries Lighthouse, Shetland, reports the occurrence of a Walrus which haunted the neighbourhood of the islands from July till October 1920, as recorded in the *Scottish Naturalist* (Nos. 107–108, 1920).

The animal was first observed early in July by the boatman and his son while lifting a fishing line inshore at the entrance of Angry Sound, when it followed the boat for some distance, about fifty yards astern.

It was subsequently seen at various times, the last being on October 13th, when it was observed by Mr Jamieson.

The tusks in this example were estimated at from 12 to 15 inches long.

According to Mr Jamieson, Walruses have been seen in the same neighbourhood twice previously during the last fifty years.

Pl. 12.

Walrus.

22

Plate 13

Family PHOCIDAE Genus HALICHOERUS

The Grey Seal
Halichoerus grypus, Fabricius
pl. 13

Until quite recent years little was known of the habits and pelage of this fine species, which was often confused with the large Bearded Seal of the Arctic seas, *Erignathus barbatus*, and we owe much to Mr Millais for the full and accurate account of its life history, which, after years of observation around our coasts, he has given in his *Mammals of Great Britain and Ireland*, vol. i. pp. 252–298. According to this authority 'four distinct types are found, as well as every intermediate form between them, that is to say, specimens may occur which are composite of two, three or even four types'. These types are described as follows: 1. The *Black* Male; 2. The *Light Grey* Male; 3. The *Blotched* Male; 4. The *Grey Spotted* Male.

The first and last mentioned are shown on the upper and lower part of Plate 13, with one of the intermediate forms between the two.

Around the throats of the adult males, and best seen in autumn when their coats are in good order, are several ridges of dark hair, forming bands which look like tarry ropes.

The colour of the female runs into two types, either light grey above and white below with some dark spots on the throat, shoulders and fore-flippers, or a dark form, chiefly composed of shades of grey, blotched and spotted with black.

A characteristic feature in nearly every example of the Grey Seal, as Mr Millais points out, is the pale grey colour of the crown of the head, which occurs in every type.

When born the young are at first pure white, and pass through various stages of colour till they gradually assume the adult coat.

The average length of the Grey Seal is about 8 feet, but some reach 9 or 9½ feet, measured from nose to end of tail.

The female measures 6 feet or thereabouts in length. The head is flatter, proportionately much longer and more like that of a dog than in the Common Seal, while the animal is not nearly as tameable and intelligent as the latter; the countenance, especially in the old males, suggesting a savage and morose disposition. On the other hand, Dr Edmonston found a young one of this species extremely gentle and affectionate.

The Grey Seal inhabits the North Atlantic, but is only sparsely distributed on the American coasts and apparently does not go farther south than Nova Scotia.

It is more abundant along the northern coasts of Europe, yet does not appear to penetrate far northwards, chiefly frequenting the shores of the North Sea, Baltic, and Gulf of Bothnia.

It is found in Iceland, the Faroes, Scandinavia and Northern Germany, and along the coasts of the British Islands.

In England it is rather rare, but a fair-sized colony inhabits the Scilly Islands, a few still exist in the Farnes, Northumberland, and from time to time it appears on other parts of our shores, as in Wales, where some are found on the coast of Pembrokeshire.

In Scotland it is much more common, especially on the north-western coast and islands, the Hebrides, Orkneys, and Shetlands.

This species is also plentiful in Ireland, where it haunts the sea-caves on many parts of the coast, chiefly along the western side.

The Grey Seal is most at home among the rough and troubled waters of our outlying islands where the sea is seldom still. There he can bask undisturbed on the shelving rocks or retire into the fastness of some cavern under water.

A typical haunt of this Seal is Rosvean, Scilly. This Seal-haunted rock lies far out to sea, fully exposed to the Atlantic rollers and is difficult to approach except in calm weather. On peeping over the high boulder-like rocks near the favourite landing-place of the animals I had three or four in full view, lying basking in the sunshine, but always watchful and ready to slip under water at the least suspicion of danger. When ashore taking their ease they appreciate a slight hollow in the rock and will often turn over and change their position to ensure more comfort. On the island of Handa, Sutherland, I

have watched for an hour or more a party of these large Seals resting on an isolated rock below the cliffs where the Fulmar Petrels and Guillemots breed. This was in the month of May when small parties will bask peaceably in company, but in the breeding season, later on in October, the big males fight fiercely and are generally much scarred as a result of these combats. Sometimes a male will occupy a sea-cave with a single female, but they are just as often polygamous. When born, the young are left on shore by the mother, who returns regularly to suckle them for the first few weeks till they take to the water.

Few animals are more difficult to obtain than the Grey Seal, owing to the stormy seas with treacherous currents where he makes his home.

Unless successfully stalked and killed instantaneously while taking his siesta near the water's edge, he is seldom secured. As a rule it is useless to shoot them while on the surface of the sea, as they sink almost immediately, and when this happens in deep water they are lost.

A successful method of capturing this Seal, which now seems to be seldom practised, was to fix a strong net under water at the entrance of the caverns frequented by the animals, when they were often caught in the toils as they tried to escape seawards.

Pl. 13.

Grey Seal. ½

Plate 14

Sub-Family PHOCINAE Genus PHOCA

The Common Seal
Phoca vitulina, Linnaeus
pl. 14

Considerably smaller than the preceding species, the adult male of the Common Seal measures from nose to end of tail from 4 to 5½ feet, or sometimes more, especially specimens from the Orkneys and Shetlands.

As shown by Mr Millais (*Mammals of Great Britain and Ireland*) there is a good deal of variation in the colour of this animal, which apart from the seasonal changes of pelage shows two distinct types, one light and the other dark, according to the closeness to each other of the dark spots and markings on the lighter ground-colour of the coat.

Between these two types intermediate forms occur. The chief figure in Plate 14 gives the lighter form in winter coat, which in August changes to a more or less plain sandy colour with only some faint markings remaining. The other and darker figures are from a younger example in the gardens of the Zoological Society of Scotland in summer.

The Common Seal is found on the coasts of the North Atlantic as well as those of the North Pacific, ranging northwards along the shores of Greenland as far as or beyond Davis Straits. It is said to frequent Spitzbergen, and also visits Iceland and the Faroes, while it is common on the coasts of northern Europe, and occasionally comes as far south as the Mediterranean.

In England this Seal is thinly distributed on the western side and scarcely known among the Scilly Islands, where the Grey Seal is not uncommon. On the east coast, some haunt the neighbourhood of the Farnes, and visit the shores of Durham, Yorkshire, and Lincolnshire, but are rare south of the Wash. In days gone by they were numerous about the sand-banks at the mouth of the Tees.

Where salmon rivers enter the sea on the east coast of Scotland the Common Seal may be seen in large numbers during the summer months, but the chief haunts of this animal in the north are the Hebrides, Orkneys, and Shetlands, where it is abundant. According to Mr Millais, in the work already quoted (vol. i. p. 310), 'the majority of those frequenting the east coast of Scotland are migratory, while those on the west are, except for local movements, stationary'.

Early in June the female gives birth to a single young one, which, unlike the pup of the Grey Seal, takes to the water almost immediately. In the opinion of Mr Millais the first white woolly coat of the baby Common Seal must be shed before birth, as there is no evidence of any ever having been observed in the water except in their second pelage.

The Common Seal, owing to the constant persecution it receives, becomes extremely wary as it gains experience, and the old male before lying up on shore for a siesta will always first carefully survey his surroundings.

One curious side of his character has been referred to by Mr Millais, who says (vol. i. p. 317): 'The look-out is often the Seal that has most recently emerged from the ocean and is still wet. From this we may deduce a certain subtle reasoning and recognition of its own limitations on the part of the animal, for only during the short time after coming from the sea is the Seal keenly alive to the possibilities of impending danger. As his coat dries he becomes too sleepy to trouble about extraneous matters, so his place must be taken by another that is more awake and fresher from the sea.'

Graceful and swift in his natural element the Seal is awkward when ashore, though capable of jerking his body forward at some speed if alarmed and making for the water. Seals are naturally inquisitive and attracted by any unusual sound, and are even credited with a love of music.

Pl. 14.

Plate 15

The Ringed Seal
Phoca hispida, Schreber
pl. 15 **left**

This small Arctic Seal, the 'Floe-rat' of the Seal hunters, usually measures about 4½ feet from nose to tip of tail.

The colour of the adult is dusky grey or brown above, curiously marked with rings and irregular figures of yellowish white, the centres of which are dark, the space round the eyes is dusky, the underparts buffish white.

The Ringed Seal penetrates far north among the ice of the circumpolar regions and has been obtained up to or beyond lat. 82°. It is common on the coasts of Greenland, Spitzbergen, Nova Zembla, North Iceland and Northern Europe, while occasional stragglers reach the British coasts.

The first recorded specimen occurred on the Norfolk coast in 1846; this was purchased in the fish market of Norwich by Mr J. H. Gurney and later indentified by Professor Flower. Mr Millais mentions two other examples, one killed at Collieston, Aberdeenshire, in August 1897, and a second taken in the salmon nets in Aberdeen Bay during the summer of 1901.

The Ringed Seal – the *netsik* of the Esquimaux hunters – forms the chief food supply of these people, as it does not leave the ice in winter. Dr Kane (*Arctic Explorations*, pp. 153–154) says 'the seal are shot lying by their *atluk* or breathing holes. As the season draws near midsummer they are more approachable: their eyes being so congested by the glare of the sun that they are sometimes nearly blind. . . . Each seal yields a liberal supply of oil, the average thus far being five gallons each. . . . The netsik will not perforate ice more than one season's growth, and are looked for therefore where there was open water the previous year.'

They pass much of their time on the ice near their breathing holes, ready to slip under water on the least alarm.

The old males have a strong offensive odour, which is said to be imparted to the Esquimaux when they eat these animals.

The Harp or Greenland Seal
Phoca groenlandica, Fabricius
pl. 15 **right**

This strikingly marked species, of which an adult male is shown in the Plate, measures from 5 to 6 feet in length.

The predominant colour is a yellowish white, with two irregular bands of deep purplish brown or black along the flanks, which meet on the shoulders.

The muzzle, face, and sides of the head are also of the same dark colour.

The females are less distinctly marked, and are often grey on the upper parts, with some dark spots.

The young, at first white, gradually acquire the adult pelage, which, according to Mr Millais, is not attained till the fifth year.

The Harp Seal inhabits the North Pacific and North Atlantic, and in spring is very abundant on the ice-fields north-east of Newfoundland, where they breed in large herds and afterwards move north to spend the summer in Greenland.

They are also found about the west coast of Greenland in autumn, and in summer are common among the floating ice around Spitzbergen and Jan Mayen.

This Seal sometimes visits the British coasts in summer, the first having been identified in 1836, when two were obtained in the Severn. Several more have been recorded from time to time, including a fine adult male, now in the Perth Museum, which was shot by Mr Kennedy while out punt-shooting in Invergowrie Bay, Carse o'Gowrie, Perthshire.

A good many other examples of the Harp Seal have been seen about the Scottish coasts and islands, while it is unlikely that any mistake could be made in identifying the species, because the clearly defined markings of the adult male may readily be recognised at a distance.

In habits the Harp Seal is migratory and gregarious. Incredible numbers collect at certain seasons among the ice-floes and are killed in thousands by professional seal hunters. The young are born on the ice in March, and when strong enough follow their parents in their migratory movements. In spite of the havoc caused by the sealers the Harp Seal is apparently as numerous as ever, according to information supplied to Mr Millais in Newfoundland. The food consists chiefly of cod and other fish.

Pl. 15.

Ringed Seal.   Harp Seal.

Plate 16

Genus ERIGNATHUS, Gill

The Bearded Seal
Erignathus barbatus, Fabricius
pl. 16 **right**

The Bearded Seal is another Arctic species which attains a large size, the adult males sometimes measuring 12 feet in length.

Dr Kane (*Arctic Explorations*, p. 154) says, 'I have measured these ten feet in length, and eight in circumference, of such unwieldy bulk as not unfrequently to be mistaken for the walrus.' Adult specimens of this Seal are rarely to be seen in British collections, the only one I have been able to find being in the Royal Scottish Museum, Edinburgh.

The coat of this example which I have figured in the Plate is of a yellowish drab-colour without spots or markings, while the flattened bristles on the muzzle, which have given the animal its name, are dull white. The head is small and round, the fore-flippers furnished with strong curved claws.

It inhabits the northern Polar Seas of both the Old and New Worlds, going far north and being well distributed from the coasts of Labrador and Greenland to Spitzbergen and the northern parts of Scandinavia. This species also frequents the North Pacific.

The Bearded Seal has only once been known with certainty to have reached the British Isles, when a young male was taken off the Norfolk coast in February 1892.

From Dr Kane we learn that this species, unlike the Ringed Seal, makes no *atluk* or breathing hole in the ice, but depends on accidental fissures where bergs or floes have been in motion. The skin is much prized by the Esquimaux for making harpoon lines for Walrus hunting.

The Hooded Seal
Cystophora cristata, Erxleben
pl. 16 **left**

The Hooded Seal, also known as the Crested Seal and Bladder-nose, measures about 8 feet in length. The drawing of this species, shown in the lower part of the Plate, was taken from a specimen in the Royal Scottish Museum.

The ground colour of the body in this example is a dark grey, blotched and marbled with black, the face and muzzle are also black.

Immature examples are silvery grey above and yellowish white below. The strange inflation on the upper parts of the face in the adult males forms a kind of bag or sac which can be filled with air when the animal is angry or excited, or relaxed when at rest.

This migrating Seal inhabits the Arctic Ocean from Greenland to Northern Europe, ranges as far north as Baffin's Bay, and also frequents the American coast.

In England the first example was taken on the River Orwell, Suffolk, in June 1847, while another was captured alive at Frodsham, Cheshire, in February 1873.

The records for Scotland are: one stoned to death by some boys on a rock near St Andrews in July 1872, one shot in Ollerswith Bay, Sanday, Orkneys, December 1890, another obtained on Benbecula in May 1891, and the last shot at the mouth of the Lossie near Elgin, in February 1903. All these seals appear to have been young animals.

Mr Millais (*Mammals of Great Britain and Ireland*, vol. i. p. 364), describes this species as loving the drift ice and rarely visiting rocky shores; he says: 'The Hooded Seals accompany the great body of the Harp Seals that come through the Straits of Belle Isle every winter, and after fishing about the Newfoundland banks, haul up on the floe ice to the east of that island, where they bring forth their young about a week later than the Harps.'

The Hooded Seal is said to be more courageous than the other species, and will defend itself or young when attacked by sealers on the ice.

Pl.16.

Hooded Seal. (adult & young)   Bearded Seal.
                        1/12

Plate 17

Family MUSTELIDAE Sub-Family LUTRINAE Genus
LUTRA

The Common Otter
Lutra vulgaris, Erxleben
pl. 17

The form of the Otter is well adapted to its aquatic habits, the long flattened body, tapering tail, short legs, and broad webbed feet enable the animal to glide silently and swiftly under water when pursuing its elusive prey. The muzzle, well provided with stiff whiskers, is broad and overlaps the lower lips. The colour of the outer hair on the upper parts is in general a rich glossy brown, while under this is a coat of soft greyish fur. The cheeks, chest, belly, and inner surface of the limbs are a dull grey. Considerable variation occurs in the size and weight of the Otter, but a full-grown male will measure from nose to end of tail from about 3½ to 4 feet, the tail being rather more than half the length of the head and body.

The Common Otter inhabits the greater part of Europe, and also Asia and America, the smaller race of Northern India and the larger one of North America not being recognised as distinct.

In the British Islands, it is widely distributed throughout England, Wales, Scotland and Ireland. Owing to its shy and retiring habits it is seldom seen except when hunted, and will often frequent a stream without its presence being detected.

The Otter usually lies up during the day in his holt or retreat, which may be under a bank, in a hollow pollard tree by the stream, or merely a dry bed among reeds or bushes, whence he issues towards nightfall to prey on various kinds of fish or on frogs. Eels form a large and favourite part of the Otter's diet, as well as salmon and grilse, while on the sea-coast numbers of flounders are caught in the shallow pools at the mouths of rivers. Occasionally small mammals and birds are eaten.

I have only once seen an Otter abroad during the day, when one passed close to me as he made his way along the banks of a rocky burn in Sutherland.

When an Otter enters the water no sound or splash will be noticed, as the animal has a wonderful power of silently gliding under the surface, leaving nothing more than a ripple and a chain of air bubbles to mark the spot where he vanished. Even the speed of the salmon is not sufficient to save it, for the Otter will persistently hunt a fish in the pools of a river until the latter is exhausted, when it is easily captured and brought ashore to be eaten. The prey is often left on the bank with nothing more than a bite taken out of the shoulder, and in former days, when Otters and salmon were plentiful in Scotland, people used regularly to visit the likely spots on the banks of rivers to obtain what the Otter had discarded.

Charles St John, who knew its habits intimately, says (*Wild Sports and Natural History of the Highlands*, 8th ed. p. 115): 'They appear to go a considerable distance, generally hunting down the stream and returning up to their place of concealment before dawn. At certain places they seem to come to land every night, or, at any rate, every time they pass that way. In solitary and undisturbed situations I have sometimes fallen in with the Otter during the day. In a loch far in the hills I have seen one raise itself half out of the water, take a steady look at me, and then sink gradually and quietly below the surface, appearing again at some distance, but next time showing only part of its head. At other times I have seen one floating down a stream with no exertion of its own which could attract notice; but passing with the current, showing only the top of its head and its nose, with its tail floating near the surface, and waving to and fro as if independent of all restraint from its owner.'

Two or three young are usually born at a time in some well-concealed shelter, such as a covered drain, a hole in a bank, or inside a hollow tree by the water. The cubs are taught to swim and catch their prey by the mother.

Otter. ♂

Plate 18

Sub-Family MELINAE Genus MELES

The Badger
Meles taxus, Boddaert
pl. 18

Our Common Badger, whose fossil remains found in ancient deposits show that his ancestors were coeval with the mammoth, appears to have some kinship with the Bear, and like that animal is plantigrade, placing the soles of the feet on the ground when moving.

The length of a full-grown Badger is about 28 to 30 inches from nose to root of tail, the latter measuring another 7 or 8 inches. The colour of the coat is chiefly a warm grizzly grey, the cheeks and forehead white, with a black band extending from near the nose to behind the ears, which are white at the tips. The throat, chest, underparts, legs, and feet are black. The thickset brawny body, powerful jaws, and long sharp claws of the Badger make him a formidable foe and a match for almost any dog large enough to enter his stronghold, and as none of our wild animals cares to molest him, he leads on the whole a peaceful life.

Our Common Badger inhabits northern Europe and Asia, and also the greater part of the British Islands, though apparently not in such numbers as formerly. However, it may often exist in a district where its presence is not suspected, owing to its nocturnal habits and love of seclusion.

It is certainly a common animal in parts of Surrey, where its earths are numerous, and from these strongholds it nightly makes forays, leaving unmistakable traces of its presence in the woods and copses, where the turf and soil have been routed by the snout of the animal while searching for grubs or roots during these evening rambles. In autumn I have often found the nests of wasps dug out and scattered, as the larvae of the insects form a favourite food of the Badger, who finds no difficulty in digging out the combs with his claws, while his thick coat effectually protects him from the stings of the insects.

The Badger takes life easily and passes a good part of it asleep in his den, though he is active enough when out at night on his rambles. His stronghold is an elaborate system of burrows dug far into the soil, and as a rule in a sloping bank, in which are various turns and corners, serving as vantage ground, where the animal can best defend itself against an enemy. Often there are several entrance tunnels to the fortress.

The Badger is scrupulously clean and tidy in his habits, and makes a comfortable bed for himself of dead bracken and grasses which is periodically replenished or sometimes taken out to air and replaced. He seldom leaves his home in the day-time, but during the short summer nights may come out about sundown.

On the whole, the Badger is a harmless and useful animal, devouring worms, grubs, reptiles, and various grubs and roots, though also partial to young rabbits, eggs, or other dainties he may come across.

With his keen power of scent he is able to detect the exact spot where a family of young rabbits have been left in their underground nursery, when he will dig directly down on them.

Though less active in winter the Badger does not hibernate, and will come out when snow covers the ground. I have seen their tracks as they left the neighbourhood of their earths, crossing a field to a distant plantation, showing where they made their nightly excursions.

Three or four young are born at a time in spring.

A. Thorburn. 1918

Badger.

Plate 19

Sub-Family MUSTELINAE Genus MUSTELA

The Pine Marten
Mustela martes, Linnaeus
pl. 19

Two species of Marten were at one time believed to inhabit the British Islands, namely the Beech Marten, *M. foina*, and the Pine Marten, *M. abietum*, as described by Bell in his *British Quadrupeds*, and it was not until 1879 that the late E. A. Alston was able to prove that we have only one, the Pine Marten.

This species differs from the white-breasted Beech Marten of the more southern parts of Continental Europe, in having a narrower skull, while the coat is darker and the breast usually orange or yellowish white. As the latter becomes paler and often white when the animal grows older, our Marten was frequently confused with the other, though not by observant naturalists like Charles St John, who long ago stated his belief that we had only one.

In colour, the outer fur of the Pine Marten is a rich glossy brown, under fur warm grey, the legs and feet a deep brown. The length of head and body about 21 inches, the tail (including hairs) 12 inches.

This species has a wide range over northern Europe and Asia, and at one time was common in many parts of the British Islands, though now much restricted in distribution and numbers.

It still lingers in the north-western districts of England and also in Wales and Ireland, while it is by no means extinct yet in the Highland deer forests, which are its chief strongholds in Scotland.

Though by nature a forest-loving species, the Pine Marten is not confined to the woods, but will often make its home among the rocky cairns and heather of the open hillside.

On such ground it preys on the mountain hare and rabbit and has been accused of killing sheep and lambs. His great agility and strength enable the Marten to surprise and overcome large birds like the blackcock, and in forest country squirrels, which are hunted down on the trees, are a favourite quarry. St John noticed its fondness for fruit, especially raspberries, and also observed that it was more often seen abroad during the day than other members of the Weasel family.

The female Marten makes use of a cairn, or sometimes the deserted nest of a bird, in which to rear her young, which usually number from two or three to five. The fur of this animal, which is closely allied to the Sable, is prized on account of its beauty, and is quite free from the unpleasant odour of the Polecat's.

Pl. 19.

Pine Marten. ½

Plate 20

The Polecat
Mustela putorius, Linnaeus
pl. 20

The Polecat, Fitchet, or Foumart (foul marten), as it is variously called, is smaller and more robust in form than the Pine Marten and is much less active and alert in character.

The length of head and body of the male measures about 18 inches, the tail 7 or 8 inches.

The under fur, soft in texture and pale yellowish buff in colour, blending with the glossy brown or black of the long outer hairs, makes a beautiful combination of colour and gives to the animal a very handsome appearance.

It owes its name of Foumart to the highly offensive odour it can emit when irritated, which is stronger than in the Stoat or Weasel.

The Polecat is found over northern and central Europe, where it occurs even high up among the Alps, but does not penetrate far into the southern parts of the Continent. In England it is rare in the southern counties and appears to be nowhere common, but, according to Mr Millais (*Mammals of Great Britain and Ireland*), it is not so rare in Wales as it is generally supposed to be.

In Scotland, where it was at one time abundant, the Polecat is now very scarce. Being very easily trapped, and preying chiefly on rabbits which it followed into their burrows, it soon became rare or extinct when steel traps became common. As it is also very destructive to game and poultry it was persistently sought for by keepers and farmers, who have more or less exterminated the species.

In character the Polecat is bold and aggressive; as an instance of this I remember as a boy one brought home by my brother, who came across the animal while eating a rat by the roadside near Dalhousie, Midlothian. On being disturbed it boldly left the shelter of the hedge and attacked, but was killed by a blow on the head with a stick.

Like the other *Mustelidae* it is very destructive and bloodthirsty, and when breaking into a hen-roost will immediately kill all the fowls within its reach.

The female is especially destructive at the time she is rearing her young, when large supplies of food, consisting of mammals, birds, and fishes, have been found in her larder. Eels and frogs appear to be a favourite food of the animal.

Pl. 20.

Polecat. ♂

Plate 21

The Stoat
Mustela erminea, Linnaeus
pl. 21 (summer)

A distinctive feature in the Stoat or Ermine, by which it can at once be recognised at all seasons, is the glossy black extremity of the tail. In summer the outer fur of the upper parts is a russet brown, the soft undercoat a pale warm grey, the lips, throat, and entire underparts, including the inside of the legs and usually the feet, are white, tinged with lemon yellow, as figured in Plate 21.

In winter in cold climates all the brown hairs on the head, body, and base of the tail generally lose their colour and become white, but show a yellow suffusion.

In Great Britain the Stoat when it whitens generally begins to change in November or December, those in the colder parts, such as northern Scotland, bleaching earlier than in England, where often the only alteration may be a slight fading of the russet coat and a small extension of the white.

According to Bell (*British Quadrupeds*, 2nd ed. pp. 198–199): 'The first indications of alteration in colour are such as might readily escape observation. It is on the basal or brown part of the tail and on the toes that the white first makes its appearance; and after this the white of the belly extends upwards on the animal's sides, thus destroying the regularity of the line where the brown and white meet; about the same time the legs become powdered with white. A more advanced stage shows the limbs and root of the tail white, and the brown of the back reduced to a narrow stripe, excepting on the rump, which, with the head and hind neck, is the latest to change; and, in fact, these parts rarely become quite white in this country.'

In Plate 22 is given a figure of the Stoat taken from the specimen obtained in Argyllshire in January 1919, which shows the full winter pelage, excepting a small mask of brown on the face, always the last part to change. As a sign that the alteration in colour is climatic and not dependent on the season, it is known that Stoats inhabiting the summit of Ben Nevis retain their white coats in summer. Some individuals seem more inclined to assume the winter dress than others, for even in the south of England I have seen one in a comparatively mild season with nearly half the body white.

The long sinuous neck and body and short legs of the Stoat are perfectly suited to its mode of life, and enable it to follow its prey such as rats into their narrow underground workings.

The average length of head and body in the male is about $10\frac{1}{2}$ inches, the tail about $5\frac{1}{2}$ or 6 inches.

In character the Stoat is the embodiment of agility and strength, and will often run down and kill animals as large as a hare, while rabbits and smaller mammals, game-birds and fowls, are also preyed on. It seems strange that such swift-footed creatures as the hare and rabbit should be unable to escape the attack of the Stoat, who kills by biting through the arteries of the neck, yet when tracked by their enemy they soon lose their nerve and lying down are easily mastered. Their despairing cries at such times are pitiful to hear.

What is still more strange is the courage sometimes displayed by a doe rabbit when her young are molested, when she will boldly charge and put to flight the aggressor. Mr Millais gives an instance of this, and I have myself witnessed a somewhat similar incident on the moors near Pitlochry, when I observed a rabbit persistently chasing a Stoat, which kept dodging among the heather in his efforts to escape.

The Stoat is naturally frolicsome, skipping about and playing for his own amusement, though he also makes use of these playful gambols to get within reach of some unsuspecting animal, whose sense of danger is lulled by his curious antics.

The Stoat is a bold and strong swimmer, and is known to be able to catch eels.

By watching his tracks in snow, sometimes in the open, or winding about hedgerows in and out of the rabbit holes, one can gain some notion of the Stoat's method of hunting and the long distances he will travel in pursuit of his quarry.

The young, usually about five or more in number, are born in a nest made in some cavity in a stone wall or bank, within a hollow tree, or sometimes in a deserted bird's nest.

In the background of Plate 21 is shown a figure of the Irish Stoat, the *Putorius hibernicus* of Mr Oldfield Thomas and Major Barrett-Hamilton; a sub-species of the Common Stoat, the chief difference being a matter of colouring.

In the Irish race the white on the upper lip is absent, and the extent of this colour is also much narrower on the belly and chest, its continuity being sometimes broken on the latter.

The measurements are rather less, whilst the white dress is seldom assumed in winter.

This form also inhabits the Isle of Man.

I am indebted to Lieut. Talbot Clifton, R.N.V.R., for kindly sending me a specimen from Connemara for the illustration.

Pl. 21.

Stoat. (summer).   Irish Stoat.

Plate 22

The Stoat
Mustela erminea, Linnaeus
pl. 22 (winter)

A distinctive feature in the Stoat or Ermine, by which it can at once be recognised at all seasons, is the glossy black extremity of the tail. In summer the outer fur of the upper parts is a russet brown, the soft undercoat a pale warm grey, the lips, throat, and entire underparts, including the inside of the legs and usually the feet, are white, tinged with lemon yellow, as figured in Plate 21.

In winter in cold climates all the brown hairs on the head, body, and base of the tail generally lose their colour and become white, but show a yellow suffusion.

In Great Britain the Stoat when it whitens generally begins to change in November or December, those in the colder parts, such as northern Scotland, bleaching earlier than in England, where often the only alteration may be a slight fading of the russet coat and a small extension of the white.

According to Bell (*British Quadrupeds*, 2nd ed. pp. 198–199): 'The first indications of alteration in colour are such as might readily escape observation. It is on the basal or brown part of the tail and on the toes that the white first makes its appearance; and after this the white of the belly extends upwards on the animal's sides, thus destroying the regularity of the line where the brown and white meet; about the same time the legs become powdered with white. A more advanced stage shows the limbs and root of the tail white, and the brown of the back reduced to a narrow stripe, excepting on the rump, which, with the head and hind neck, is the latest to change; and, in fact, these parts rarely become quite white in this country.'

In Plate 22 is given a figure of the Stoat taken from the specimen obtained in Argyllshire in January 1919, which shows the full winter pelage, excepting a small mask of brown on the face, always the last part to change. As a sign that the alteration in colour is climatic and not dependent on the season, it is known that Stoats inhabiting the summit of Ben Nevis retain their white coats in summer. Some individuals seem more inclined to assume the winter dress than others, for even in the south of England I have seen one in a comparatively mild season with nearly half the body white.

The long sinuous neck and body and short legs of the Stoat are perfectly suited to its mode of life, and enable it to follow its prey such as rats into their narrow underground workings.

The average length of head and body in the male is about $10\frac{1}{2}$ inches, the tail about $5\frac{1}{2}$ or 6 inches.

In character the Stoat is the embodiment of agility and strength, and will often run down and kill animals as large as a hare, while rabbits and smaller mammals, game-birds and fowls, are also preyed on. It seems strange that such swift-footed creatures as the hare and rabbit should be unable to escape the attack of the Stoat, who kills by biting through the arteries of the neck, yet when tracked by their enemy they soon lose their nerve and lying down are easily mastered. Their despairing cries at such times are pitiful to hear.

What is still more strange is the courage sometimes displayed by a doe rabbit when her young are molested, when she will boldly charge and put to flight the aggressor. Mr Millais gives an instance of this, and I have myself witnessed a somewhat similar incident on the moors near Pitlochry, when I observed a rabbit persistently chasing a Stoat, which kept dodging among the heather in his efforts to escape.

The Stoat is naturally frolicsome, skipping about and playing for his own amusement, though he also makes use of these playful gambols to get within reach of some unsuspecting animal, whose sense of danger is lulled by his curious antics.

The Stoat is a bold and strong swimmer, and is known to be able to catch eels.

By watching his tracks in snow, sometimes in the open, or winding about the hedgerows in and out of the rabbit holes, one can gain some notion of the Stoat's method of hunting and the long distances he will travel in pursuit of his quarry.

The young, usually about five or more in number, are born in a nest made in some cavity in a stone wall or bank, within a hollow tree, or sometimes in a deserted bird's nest.

In the background of Plate 21 is shown a figure of the Irish Stoat, the *Putorius hibernicus* of Mr Oldfield Thomas and Major Barrett-Hamilton; a sub-species of the Common Stoat, the chief difference being a matter of colouring.

In the Irish race the white on the upper lip is absent, and the extent of this colour is also much narrower on the belly and chest, its continuity being sometimes broken on the latter.

The measurements are rather less, whilst the white dress is seldom assumed in winter.

This form also inhabits the Isle of Man.

I am indebted to Lieut. Talbot Clifton, R.N.V.R., for kindly sending me a specimen from Connemara for the illustration.

Pl. 22.

Stoat. (winter). ♂

Plate 23

The Weasel
Mustela vulgaris, Erxleben
pl. 23

Apart from its short and comparatively slender tail, of a uniform reddish brown in colour without any black at the tip, the Weasel may be readily distinguished from the Stoat by its smaller size, paler colour, and pure white underparts.

In length of head and body the male measures about 8 inches, with 2 inches more for the tail. The female is less, often so much so that it has been mistaken for a smaller species, and in the southern counties of England was known as the 'Cane' or 'Kine'.

The Weasel inhabits Europe, northern and central Asia, and North America.

Though common throughout the mainland of Great Britain it is unknown in Ireland, where the only species of the *Mustelidae* are the Marten and Stoat, but the latter often passes under the name of 'Weasel' in Ireland.

On account of its fondness for mice, voles, and young rats, the Weasel deserves the benediction of all farmers and agriculturists, and well repays protection. It is not nearly so destructive to game as the Stoat or Polecat, though showing a decided partiality for young rabbits.

Mouse holes and the tunnels of moles are easily entered by this slim little hunter, and as he hunts by scent his prey seldom escapes.

When after a mouse or vole the Weasel follows along their runs without a check; I have watched one chasing a vole, which was first hunted out of a hedgebank, and killed as it tried to cross the open road by a single bite on the head.

As far as I have noticed, voles when hunted do not lie down and give in like a hare or rabbit, but do their best to escape till the end.

Weasels can climb well and will ascend a tree to some height. I once dislodged one from a Martin's nest under the eaves of my house, which was apparently used as a snug day-time retreat by the Weasel.

The hearing and scenting powers of this animal seem much better than its eyesight, and if the sound of a mouse in distress is imitated by a squeaking noise of the lips, a Weasel may be lured to within the distance of a yard or two. I have seen one come close up to me on a high road.

Instances have been known of birds of prey being killed in the air by the bites of Weasels on which they had pounced. Bell mentions an encounter of this sort, when a Kite had been the aggressor.

Like the Stoat, the Weasel will occasionally hunt in company, when small packs of half a dozen or so will work together like hounds. These parties probably consist of the mother and her grown-up family.

As an instance of the tiny space through which a Weasel can pass its slender body, I once found one in a mole trap with its body behind the shoulders encircled by the small perforated piece of metal which acts as a trigger, the aperture being only about an inch in diameter.

The five or six young are born in a nest placed in a hole in a wall or old tree.

In the northern parts of its range in Europe and America the Weasel is said to become entirely white in winter, but this change of colour does not occur in Great Britain, where the white examples recorded from time to time appear to be albinos.

Pl. 23.

Weasel. ⅔

Plate 24

Order RODENTIA, rodents, or gnawing animals
Family SCIURIDAE Genus SCIURUS

The Common Squirrel
Sciurus vulgaris, Linnaeus
pl. 24

Passing the greater part of its life among the branches of trees, the strong flexible feet and sharp claws of the Squirrel enable it to maintain a hold of the boughs with the greatest ease, whilst the long bushy tail, besides acting as a poise for the body, forms a warm wrap against the cold.

The length of the head and body is about 8¾ inches, the tail, including the hairs, about 8½ inches.

When in full winter coat, which is assumed in October by a moult, the colour of the fur is in general a soft warm grey, as shown in the Plate, relieved by the chestnut tints on the limbs and white underparts, which do not change with the season. The tail, rather flat than cylindrical in form, is well haired, bushy, and glossy brown in colour with a pale buff tip.

In summer the coat moults again to a more or less reddish chestnut hue, and the hairs of the tail, which by this time are scanty, blanch to a light buff colour. Blyth appears to have been the first to observe that the Squirrel sheds its coat twice in the year, and that in summer the ornamental ear-tufts are entirely wanting.

The Common Squirrel inhabits Europe from Lapland to northern Italy, and ranges throughout Siberia to Japan.

Those in the more northern parts of its habitat are very grey in colour and provide a valuable fur.

In England, Wales, and Scotland, the Squirrel is indigenous and common in most wooded districts, but in Ireland, where it is also plentiful, it is said to have been introduced by human agency in quite recent times.

This nimble little climber is familiar to most of us in the country, as he passes from tree to tree among the topmost branches or swiftly runs up their stems in a nervous jerky manner when surprised upon the ground.

Mr Millais, in his *Mammals of Great Britain and Ireland* (vol. ii. pp. 147–148), has most happily described its acrobat-like behaviour as follows: 'Often after its first rush to safety it lies flat and motionless against the trunk with all legs extended and head pressed close to the bark. If you follow it round to get a better view, it either ascends by scrambling rushes to the higher branches, or, if it considers the tree too bare, darts off along the stems to another and yet another tree, until it finds refuge high up in some dense pine or Scotch fir, where it is lost to sight. In such a position it will remain for hours without moving. When running from one tree to another it keeps its tail depressed, and it uses this appendage with great skill to aid in maintaining its balance when running along the slender twigs.'

The food of the Squirrel is varied, consisting chiefly of nuts and other seeds of trees, wild berries, the eggs and young of birds, and also the old birds when it can catch them.

One on a spruce fir in my garden was seen to take a flying leap at a small bird – a robin, I think – which, however, it failed to secure.

Gilbert White observed that the Squirrel when eating a nut, after rasping off the small end, splits the shell in two with his long foreteeth, as a man does with his knife.

Stores of beech-mast and nuts are laid by in some hiding place for the winter, and during this time the Squirrel sleeps a good deal in his warm winter 'drey' or nest, but it seems doubtful whether the animal hibernates much at this season, in Britain at all events. One sees them abroad even in the coldest weather, and the scattered remains of fir cones on the snow under the trees show where they have been feeding.

Early in spring a nesting drey is prepared, in which from two to four young are born at a time.

Pl. 24.

Squirrel ⅔

Plate 25

Family MYOXIDAE Genus MUSCARDINUS

The Common Dormouse
Muscardinus avellanarius, Linnaeus
pl. 25

Allied to the Squirrel, which it resembles in some of its habits, the Dormouse is of stouter build than the true mice and possesses a thicker and bushy tail.

The prevailing colour of this attractive little animal is a soft brownish buff, brighter on the face and flanks, blending into pale cream colour on the belly, and white on the throat and breast. The fur is very soft in texture, with a beautiful grey gloss or bloom on the upper parts of the body.

The length from nose to root of tail in a full-grown specimen is about 3 inches, the tail between 2½ and 3 inches. The large prominent dark eye is a striking feature in this beautiful species.

The Dormouse is more restricted in his distribution than the Squirrel, inhabiting central Europe from northern Italy to Sweden and ranging eastwards to Galicia.

In the British Islands its range is confined to England and Wales, where it is unevenly distributed and does not appear to be known farther than the northern boundaries of Durham.

The Dormouse is fairly plentiful in the southern and western counties of England, though rare in the Midlands and Norfolk. A full account of its distribution has been given by Mr G. T. Rope in the *Zoologist*, June 1885.

I have found it abundant in the neighbourhood of Godalming in Surrey, where the numerous copses of hazelnut, shady hedgerows and similar cover seem specially suited to its habits. Mr Millais in his work on our Mammals has pointed out the 'great similarity in the habitat of this animal and the nightingale. Both frequent forest edges but seem to shun the solitude of the forest itself.'

Having fattened on the autumnal harvest of nuts, the Dormouse lays by a store for the winter and retires to its nest about the latter part of October, when curling itself into a ball, with the tail wrapping the head and body, it falls into a deep slumber which lasts with a few short intervals of partial activity till the following April.

The winter nest, composed of dead grasses, leaves, and moss, is variously placed, sometimes among roots or ivy-covered stumps of trees close to the ground, sometimes in thickets of brambles, where the one shown in the Plate was situated. I have seen it built near the top of a haystack at some distance from the ground, and also in a clump of bamboo, where the dead leaves of the plant had been used for the fabric.

A captive Dormouse which I once kept as a model, escaping in my room, made a dormitory for itself in the canvas of a sketching umbrella, where I found it fast asleep.

Although apparently sluggish in temperament, the Dormouse at times shows wonderful agility, leaping from branch to branch in a hedge in a surprising manner, and catching hold of the twigs with great dexterity. It is also good-tempered and seldom bites when handled. In habits this animal is mostly nocturnal, though it will sometimes come out in daylight.

The food consists chiefly of various wild fruits and nuts, whilst insects and grubs are also eaten.

The female produces three or four young at a time in a nursery built for the purpose usually quite near the ground. This is larger than the dormitory made by the Dormouse as a retreat in summer.

Various local names have been given to this animal, such as Sleeper, Sleep-mouse, Seven-sleeper, etc., all descriptive of its hibernating habits.

Pl. 25.

Dormouse. $\frac{3}{4}$.

Plate 26

Family MURIDAE Sub-Family MURINAE Genus MUS

The Harvest Mouse
Mus minutus, Pallas
pl. 26 **top**

The Harvest Mouse has several characteristic features which distinguish it from the rest of the genus. It is by far the smallest and also the brightest in colour of our mice, measuring in length of head and body from 2¼ to about 2½ inches, the tail being about 2¼ inches long. The slim and delicate form, rather blunt nose, short and rounded ears and small eyes, as well as the faculty it possesses of grasping things with the tail, all serve to distinguish this species.

In colour the upper parts are chiefly golden brown, blending into a tawny orange tint about the region of the tail. The underparts are white, with the dividing line well defined.

The young are duller in colour, which is usually described as resembling that of the House Mouse, but one I have seen in early autumn was more or less of a sandy buff.

The Harvest Mouse inhabits the greater part of Continental Europe, but is not known south of the Pyrenees nor farther north than Finland. Eastwards it reaches China and Japan.

We are indebted to Gilbert White of Selborne for the earliest written account of this species in England, as described in a letter to Pennant in November 1767, but Montagu claims to have known it in Wiltshire before its discovery in Hampshire by the Selborne naturalist.

Though the Harvest Mouse is now undoubtedly less plentiful than in former days, perhaps, as has been suggested, on account of the closely cut stubble left by the modern reaping machine, it seems still to be well distributed over the greater part of England, especially in the southern and eastern divisions.

Though I have never succeeded in finding the nest, I consider the species fairly common in the neighbourhood of Godalming, Surrey, having in January 1918 received seven specimens and later in the same winter some others, which had been obtained when corn stacks were threshed.

In the Midland counties it seems to be rarer, and from Yorkshire northwards it becomes still less frequent, records from the Lake district, Durham, and Northumberland being few and far between.

Across the border in Scotland it has only occurred locally and at rare intervals. MacGillivray recorded it from Aberdeenshire, Midlothian, and Fifeshire, and in the last mentioned county found a nest in a tuft of grass (*aira coespitosa*). Mr W. Evans recorded a nest discovered by himself near Aberlady, East Lothian. The Harvest Mouse has also been noted in Berwickshire, Renfrewshire, Ayrshire, Kirkcudbrightshire, and a few other counties at different times.

The question whether it inhabits Wales is uncertain and it is unknown in Ireland.

During the warmer part of the year this species lives amidst the tall vegetation of hedgerows, in reed-beds, or in fields of growing corn, where, woven among the wheat or barley stalks, grass stems, or thistle heads, the nest may be found, skilfully fashioned of grasses, corn blades, etc. The interior is lined with finely shredded leaves of grasses or other plants.

Gilbert White noted that one found suspended in the head of a thistle in a wheat field was 'most artificially platted, and composed of the blades of wheat, perfectly round and about the size of a cricket ball, with the aperture so ingeniously closed that there was no discovering to what part it belonged. It was so complete and well filled that it would roll across the table without being discomposed, though it contained eight little mice that were naked and blind.'

The Harvest Mouse breeds several times in the year, producing from five to about eight or nine young at a time.

In England this species usually shelters in corn stacks during winter, but in Holland, according to the late Professor Schlegel, they make their winter nests among reed-beds. These differ from their summer homes, being larger and composed of mosses, and resembling the nest of the Reed Warbler in their attachment to the stems of the plants, not far from the water's level.

The Harvest Mouse is occasionally active and about in winter. I have had one which was caught in a hedgerow near my home in December, and at another time I got a specimen from a stable, which had probably been brought in with some straw.

Though slower in movement and without the power of leaping like the Field Mouse, they are nimble little creatures, and climb among the corn stalks and stems of grasses with an easy action, assisted as they pause in passing from one straw to another by their more or less prehensile tails, which instinctively lapping round a stalk, help to steady the foothold of the animal.

The food consists of corn and seeds of various kinds and also, it has often been observed, of insects. Two of these mice I watched for some time in captivity were very clever in catching any small flies which entered their cage, when they were promptly seized and eaten.

These mice make interesting and cleanly little pets, and soon get accustomed to captivity.

The Wood Mouse
Mus sylvaticus, Linnaeus
pl. 26 **bottom**

The Wood Mouse, also known as the Field Mouse or Long-tailed Field Mouse, is subject to great variation in size and colour which has led modern naturalists to sub-divide it into many local varieties or sub-species. It is one of the most common and widely distributed of British mammals.

The prevalent form inhabiting our islands (the *Mus sylvaticus intermedius* of Millais) has in general a length in head and body of 3⅝ inches, with about the same measurement for the tail. The colour of the upper parts is a yellowish brown, brighter on the cheeks and along the lower part of the ribs, and shaded with blackish hairs which are most distinct about the back. The basal portion of the fur is dark slate colour. The underparts are white or greyish white with usually a breast-spot of a buffish tint. The feet are light greyish flesh colour.

The young are always much greyer and duller in colour.

This species is easily distinguished from the Common House Mouse, apart from its brighter colouring, by the large prominent black eyes and much longer ears, hind legs, and tail. In general, the Wood Mouse has also a more thoroughbred look than the other.

Wood Mice, not differing from the typical British form, as well as other races, are found over the greater part of Europe.

Throughout the British islands this species has a widespread distribution, and various local races, showing more or less some difference in size and colour, have been differentiated to such an extent that almost every island off the west coast of Scotland, as well as the Shetlands and Fair Isle, appear to have their own race of Field Mouse.

The Wood Mouse inhabits fields, hedgerows, gardens and woodlands, as well as districts devoid of trees, and even the seashore.

Though nocturnal in habits, it may sometimes be seen by day, and, as like other mice it seems to be shortsighted, it may often be watched at close quarters when the observer remains still. Being an excellent climber it obtains much of its food, especially in autumn, among the branches of various hedgerow bushes and trees, such as the hawthorn, wild rose, and others on whose fruit it feeds. Old nests of birds are often used by the mice as platforms or tables on which they place their food, and when these are not conveniently at hand I have seen large collections of the red pulp and empty seeds of hips left on the ground. These are usually nipped off whole and carried to the dining table, though I have noticed the rinds left on the trees with the seeds only removed.

The Wood Mouse is very destructive to crocus and other bulbs in flower beds, and also eats insects and at times even the flesh of its own kind.

The female breeds several times in the year, and produces from about four to six young at a time.

Sometimes the nursery, consisting of a domed nest made of grasses, is placed above ground, but more often it is built inside a burrow. Though this species does not appear to hibernate in winter, it prepares a snug hiding place for the cold weather. I have known a Wood Mouse to have two winter retreats close together, one made of moss in a thorn hedge, and

62

continued on page 64

Pl. 26.

Harvest Mouse.

Wood Mouse. $\frac{3}{4}$

Plate 27

British Yellow-necked Wood Mouse
Mus sylvaticus wintoni, Barrett-Hamilton
pl. 27 **top**

This handsome variety, first recognized by Mr De Winton and described by him in 1894, is of large size and bright colouring; with a well marked band of pale yellowish buff across the chest. The centre of this branches upwards and downwards, and forms a kind of cross. An adult male has a total length from nose to tip of tail of 8¾ inches, the tail being usually the same length as the head and body combined. The hind feet and legs are very large and strong. The ears are also large and beautifully modelled, suggesting in their delicate outlines the structure of some sea shell.

This mouse is very strong and active, and can leap to a considerable height.

It is common in Surrey, where, as in other districts, it seems to occur more frequently in houses and garden sheds than elsewhere, though owing to its strictly nocturnal habits its presence out of doors may pass unnoticed. Every winter I catch numbers in a loft in my house where the Common Wood Mouse seldom appears, but I have never known it to enter inhabited rooms. Apples are a great attraction to it in winter.

The figures in the Plate were drawn from a pair I kept in captivity. From my own experience the chief plunderers of early sown peas are the Common Wood Mouse and not De Winton's.

The St Kilda Field Mouse
Mus sylvaticus hirtensis, Barrett-Hamilton
pl. 27 **bottom**

This is another very large sub-species, but less brightly coloured than the one last described. The largest of a number of specimens, obtained by Dr Eagle Clarke on the St Kilda group of islands in the Autumns of 1910 and 1911, measured in length of head and body 129 millimetres, the tail 100 millimetres, making the total length of the animal from nose to tip of tail about 9 inches. The following is from his description of this fine mouse in the *Scottish Naturalist* (June 1914), 'The St Kilda Field Mouse is confined to the main island Hirta, and to the adjacent uninhabited isles of Soay and Dun. It is most abundant where coarse grass prevails, but is to be found almost everywhere – in the crofted area, in the neighbourhood of the houses, on the faces of the cliffs, and on the sides and hilltops; finding congenial retreats in the rough stone-built "cleits" (which are such a feature in the St Kilda landscape) and in the walls surrounding the crofts'. . . . 'That the underparts of *hirtensis* are heavily washed with yellowish brown has hitherto been deemed an important characteristic of the species. This in not the case, however, for in the *majority* of adult specimens, and many of the immature ones, the throat, chest, and abdomen are white, and only washed with brown along the narrow medium ventral line. As a result, the demarcation between the peppery reddish-brown upper, and the pale under surface is pronounced in most examples, and renders the species very similar to the familiar Long-tailed Field Mouse (*Apodemus sylvaticus*). About one-third of the adults and the majority of the younger specimens have the under surface more or less strongly washed with yellowish brown.'

The figure in the Plate was drawn from one of the specimens obtained by Dr Eagle Clarke.

The Hebridean Field Mouse
Mus sylvaticus hebridensis, W. E. De Winton
(not shown)

This variety is larger and more stoutly built than the Common Wood Mouse and has also longer feet and shorter ears.

In colour there is less distinction between the upper and underparts, the latter being duller and strongly suffused with buff, with a patch of this colour on the chest. It appears to be confined to Lewis and Barra, Outer Hebrides, and was first discovered by Mr J. Steele Elliot and described later by Mr W. E. De Winton.

The Irish Wood Mouse
Mus sylvaticus celticus, Barrett-Hamilton
(not shown)

This is a small race about the size of *Mus sylvaticus*, with dark upper parts and white on the under side, inhabiting the south and west of Ireland and also the Hebrides and Skye.

---

continued from Plate 26

The Wood Mouse

the other consisting of a burrow in the ground just below.

When disturbed it would leap from its retreat in the bushes and take refuge in the hole underground.

The Wood Mouse is a favourite prey for Owls, Kestrels, Weasels, and other predatory animals.

Pl.27.

Yellow-necked Wood Mouse.

St. Kilda Wood Mouse 3/4

Plate 28

The Common Mouse or House Mouse
Mus musculus, Linnaeus
pl. 28

Smaller than the Wood Mouse, this species is easily distinguished from the other by its dull and more uniform colour, small beady eyes, and shorter ears and tail. The whiskers are also neither so long nor so plentiful.

The head and body of the adult measure about $3\frac{1}{2}$ inches, the tail about $3\frac{1}{4}$ inches.

The colour of the fur in the upper parts is a dusky brownish grey, fading into grey on the sides and belly. The Common Mouse is subject to considerable variation of colour, those living an outdoor life away from houses having usually a more sandy hue than their indoor relations, while black, dark brown, white, or spotted examples are not uncommon. Some local varieties have been noticed on the Scottish Islands, the most distinct being the House Mouse of St Kilda.

As far as we know the Common Mouse had its origin in Asia, whence it spread into Europe in prehistoric times.

It usually makes a home for itself in dwelling houses and will quietly enter new premises even before the building is completed. Breeding many times in the year and producing half-a-dozen young at a time, it increases enormously under favourable conditions, and like the Brown Rat soon becomes a plague if not kept within bounds. Great damage is done by mice in corn ricks, where they will often collect in hundreds. It is less nocturnal in its habits than the Wood Mouse and will often come out in daylight when in search of attractive food.

The Common Mouse is a good climber and with its power of gnawing soon finds a way into cupboards and storerooms, where it will often make its nest and rear its young. The nest is made of various warm materials, including odds and ends of wool, straw, shreds of paper, etc.

This species seems sensitive to cold, and, like the Wood Mouse, when caught alive in a trap during chilly weather and not quickly removed, will soon become numb and die from exposure.

The most distinctly marked variety of this Mouse in the British Islands is the St Kilda House Mouse (*Mus muralis*, Barrett-Hamilton) whose head and body measure up to $4\frac{3}{8}$ inches and tail nearly $3\frac{5}{8}$ inches. The example shown in Plate 28 was drawn from a specimen obtained along with a number of others by Dr Eagle Clarke for the Royal Scottish Museum, who describes it as follows in the *Scottish Naturalist* (June 1914), 'This is the House Mouse of St Kilda, and being such is not found out of Hirta – the only inhabited isle of the group. On this island, however, it is not confined to the houses, where it is very abundant, but occurs in the crofts, finding shelter in the walls and cleits. . . .

'In general colour the upper surface of all the adults resembles that of a rather light-coloured example of the ordinary House Mouse; but the coloration of the upper [apparently "under" is meant] surface presents a remarkable departure from that species, being of a bright buff and clearly separated from the upper surface by a well marked line of demarcation. The hind foot is broader and more robust than in *Mus musculus*.'

Pl.28.

St. Kilda House Mouse.

Common Mouse.

Plate 29

The Black Rat
Mus rattus, Linnaeus
pl. 29

The so-called 'Black' Rat is a smaller and less heavily built animal than the common Brown Rat, and is characterised by its comparatively slender head and body, large shapely ears, and long tail. The measurements are, head and body about 7½ inches, tail about 8½, but individuals vary a good deal in size.

This animal, usually known as the 'Old English Black Rat', has not been quite happily named, as the colour can hardly be called black and its origin is certainly not English.

Whence it first came appears uncertain but it probably originated, as a more brightly coloured form, in Southern Asia, and travelling westwards by degrees, is supposed to have been brought to Europe in the ships of the Crusaders during the eleventh and twelfth centuries, where it soon established itself and began to attract attention.

The species is not mentioned by the ancient Greek or Roman writers.

In time the colder climate of Europe seems to have changed the originally brighter coloration to a much darker hue.

In England, where this Rat was known as early as the thirteenth century, it was not long in becoming a permanent and unwelcome guest, and continued as the only British species until the coming of the larger Brown Rat (*Mus decumanus*), early in the eighteenth century. The latter, owing to its superior strength, resourceful character, and greater prolificacy, soon ousted the weaker race when they came in contact, until the old Black Rat became scarce and nearly extinct throughout the greater part of the country, except in some of the seaports. However, this species being by nature well adapted to a life on board ship, has often been able to re-establish itself in small colonies from overseas, as in Yarmouth, where it was found to be numerous by Mr A. H. Paterson in 1896. Colonies occur in London about the docks, also in Bristol and Sunderland, and it has long been known in the Channel Islands.

The Black Rat was plentiful in Scotland well into the nineteenth century, being common at one time in both the Orkneys and Shetlands.

Compared with the Brown Rat, this species is more active and better adapted for climbing and is said to inhabit by preference the upper parts of houses, while its larger cousins remain below in the drains and cellars.

The Black Rat is less cunning and suspicious than the other. Both have an evil reputation as spreaders of plague and other diseases. The present species breeds several times each year, from seven to nine young being born at a time in a warm nest made of various materials.

Mr Millais considers there are in the British Islands three well-marked races of the so-called 'Black Rat', which he names the Alexandrine Rat (figured in Plate 29), the Northern Alexandrine Rat, *i.e.* the misnamed 'Old English Black Rat' (also figured in the Plate), and the Black Alexandrine Rat. The first mentioned he regards 'as undoubtedly the true species of which the last named are sub-specific races'.

The colour of the upper parts of the Alexandrine Rat is a dull yellowish brown, shaded along the back with long dark hairs; the underparts are yellowish white.

In colour, the 'Old English Black Rat' has the upper parts of a glistering slaty black, the under surface being a leaden grey, while the Black Alexandrine Rat, described as a recent arrival on our shores, really deserves its name on account of its glossy coat, jet black above and rather lighter below. Mr Millais informs us that this race 'is a native of the Black Sea ports, although its original home is, like that of the other races, unknown. Its habits are similar, and it is a great traveller on board the grain ships, and has doubtless reached many out-of-the-way places of which at present we are ignorant.' Differing in colour only, the three forms are identical in shape and habits and will freely interbreed when they come in contact with each other.

Pl. 29.

Alexandrine Rat.   Black Rat.   ⅔

Plate 30

The Brown Rat
Mus decumanus, Pallas
pl. 30

The Brown or Common Rat, known also as 'Norway Rat' and 'Hanoverian Rat', is too familiar to require much description, and is distinguished from the Black Rat by its stouter form, rounder head and muzzle, smaller ears, and comparatively short and more scaly tail. The whiskers are also less plentiful and not so long.

The colour above is a tawny greyish brown, darkened with numerous black hairs along the ridge of the back, the under-parts are dull white. Full grown specimens vary much in size, but they often attain a length of 9 inches in the head and body, and 7½ inches in the tail.

An exceptionally large example examined by Mr Millais in Sussex had a total length from nose to tip of tail of 19½ inches, and another has been recorded of 23 inches.

The original habitat of this species, like that of the Black Rat, is uncertain, but the more temperate parts of Siberia are considered to have been an ancient nursery of the race.

According to Pallas the species moved westwards in hordes in 1727. Invading Russia and other neighbouring countries, it appeared in England before 1730, where it soon settled down and rapidly increased in numbers, but did not reach Scotland till after 1764.

No other animal is so deservedly unpopular as the Common Rat. Universally hated and with every man's hand against it, it nevertheless contrives to exist and increase in numbers in spite of all the traps, poison, and other devices invented for its destruction. Whether recent legislation making it compulsory for owners of property to clear their premises of these mischievous creatures, will prove effective or not, remains to be seen.

The annual amount of damage caused by the consumption and spoiling of all kinds of food and stores by Rats is beyond calculation, apart from the destruction caused by their gnawing and burrowing propensities, which enable them to undermine the structure of houses and other buildings.

In a little book entitled *Rats and Mice as the Enemies of Mankind* (2nd ed. 1920), by M. A. C. Hinton, printed by order of the Trustees of the British Museum, an appalling account is given of the loss annually caused in Great Britain by Rats, which is put as high as £15,000,000 by some authorities.

The fleas infesting Rats are the chief cause of the spreading of plague and other diseases, as these insects carry the *bacillus* from the infected animals to man, so the danger to health is quite as serious as the material loss.

Possessed of great cunning and intelligence as well as courage, the old and experienced Rat is seldom outwitted, but the half-grown young will often crowd into a trap when once one has entered.

Though sometimes coming out in the daytime, the Rat is chiefly nocturnal in habits, and, as twilight approaches, may be seen leaving his underground retreat in search of a meal, when nothing edible escapes attention.

He flourishes in large cities as well as on uninhabited islands off our coasts, where he subsists on shellfish or garbage thrown up by the sea.

The female produces several litters in the year, about thirteen or fourteen young being born at a time, which accounts for the rapid increase of the animal.

When asleep, the Rat curls its body into a ball with the forehead placed on the ground and the nose tucked under the chest and between the forepaws.

A dark variety of the Common Rat, entirely black in colour except for a patch of white on the breast, was first observed in Ireland and described by Thompson in 1837, who considered it nearly allied to the Black Rat (*Mus rattus*). It has since been shown to be merely a melanistic form of *Mus decumanus*, which occurs in the Outer Hebrides and also in various English counties, where it appears to be spreading in increased numbers.

Pl.30.

Brown Rat. $\frac{2}{3}$

Plate 31

Sub-Family MICROTINAE

The Bank Vole
Evotomys glareolus, Schreber
pl. 31 **top**

Compared with the true mice, the distinctive character of the Voles lies chiefly in their short and rounded head, small eyes, short ears and tail, and a general stoutness of form caused by the thick and furry coat.

Four species inhabit Great Britain, namely, the Bank Vole, the Field Vole, the Orkney Vole, and the Water Vole, while various sub-species have been noted.

The most mouse-like of this group in character and form is the Bank Vole, which shows considerable variation in size, English specimens being usually rather smaller than those of Scotland.

An adult male taken in Surrey measured from nose to root of tail barely $3\frac{5}{8}$ inches, the tail alone $1\frac{13}{16}$ inches.

The colour of the upper parts in autumn and winter is a dark rusty brown, greyer on the flanks. The cheeks and underparts are grey, but often tinged with pale buff in the centre of the chest and belly. The feet are brownish grey. In summer the russet hue on the back is much brighter.

This species is widely distributed in Europe and Asia.

It was first described in England by Yarrell in 1832 and was soon found to inhabit a wide area in Great Britain. In Scotland it attracted the attention of MacGillivray before 1838, but for many years it was considered a rather uncommon species in places where it is now known to be plentiful.

As with other Voles, it does not occur in Ireland.

I have found it to be extremely common throughout the year near Godalming in Surrey, where every winter numbers enter my house; these however confine themselves to lofts under the tiles or to outhouses. They are easily trapped, as, like the Wood Mouse, the Bank Vole is very unsuspicious.

Although of nocturnal habits it may often be seen abroad during the day sitting on its haunches while nibbling bulbs and shoots of plants, or creeping among the ivy or withered leaves in hedgerows, which are a favourite resort and often quite undermined by their complicated runs.

I have observed that this species is very fond of flower borders, especially those which are backed by loose stone walls overgrown with plants, where it has a safe retreat at hand in the cracks and openings, and a varied supply of vegetable food among the beds.

The Bank Vole lives chiefly on the seeds and shoots of plants; it is also fond of fruit, especially apples, and will gnaw the tender bark of young trees.

In general its habits are much the same as the Field Vole's, but it is less of a vegetarian and more alert and quick in its actions than the other. It will eat insects, snails, young birds, and other animal food and is also addicted to cannibalism. I have found the partially eaten remains of one in a trap set among apples on a shelf, and soon afterwards caught another of the same species close to what was left of the first.

As an instance of the boldness of this little animal, Mr A. H. Cocks, writing in the *Field* (January 25th, 1919) describes how he once witnessed one attacking a young rabbit, about six times the bulk of its aggressor, which had been badly injured by a mowing machine.

A large and brightly coloured form of the Bank Vole, known as the Skomer Vole (*Evotomys hercynicus Skomerensis*, Millais), confined to Skomer Island, off the coast of Pembrokeshire, Wales, is considered by Mr Millais as only a sub-species.

This is considerably larger than the Common Bank Vole, measuring about $4\frac{1}{4}$ inches in length of head and body and about $2\frac{3}{16}$ inches in the tail.

The colour of the upper parts is a fine orange brown, becoming duller and paler on the cheeks and flanks and greyish white tinged with buff on the underparts. The Skomer Vole was first discovered by Mr Drane of Cardiff when he visited the island of that name in 1897.

At this time, according to Mr Millais (*Mammals of Great Britain and Ireland*), Mr Drane 'caught several specimens and partially described them in a paper which he read before the Cardiff Naturalists' Society, and which was published in their "Transactions".'

Later, in 1906, the Skomer Vole was fully described by the late Major Barrett-Hamilton, who gives it full specific rank.

Mr Drane observed that the Skomer and Bank Vole are much alike in their general character and habits, and though both frequent the neighbourhood of farmsteads, the former shows a decided preference for such localities, where it may be found in numbers in and around the buildings. Winter stores of turnips are a favourite resort of the Skomer and Bank Vole.

Mr Drane found that the Skomer Vole bred freely in captivity, five specimens, which soon grew tame, having produced forty-seven young in one season.

A comparatively large race of Bank Vole, possessing rather short ears and tail (*Evotomys alstoni*, Barrett-Hamilton and Hinton), inhabits the Island of Mull, Scotland. Specimens were first taken there by Mr R. W. Sheppard in June 1912. In colour the upper parts of this variety are a deep reddish brown, the underparts yellowish.

Another large form (*Evotomys erica*, Barrett-Hamilton and Hinton), closely related to the one inhabiting Mull, has been found among heather on the Island of Raasay, which lies between Skye and the mainland. Describing this vole, Major Barrett-Hamilton says (*A History of British Mammals*, p. 425): 'Unlike *E. alstoni*, but in this respect resembling *skomerensis* and *caesarius*, it has undergone considerable specialisation, apparently to fit it for subsistence upon a coarser and probably more exclusively vegetarian diet.' The colour of the upper parts is dark brown, the underparts are strongly tinted with buff.

The Common Field Vole
Microtus agrestis, Linnaeus
pl. 31 **left**

This species may be distinguished at a glance from the Bank Vole by its larger and rounder head, blunter muzzle, and by the ears being more or less concealed by the fur. The tail is also much shorter and the colour duller.

The average length of the head and body is about 4 inches, that of the tail about $1\frac{1}{4}$ inches.

The general colour of the upper parts is a greyish brown, the under surface dull white or grey. Some individuals are brighter than others, with a more russet tinge on the back.

There are few cultivated areas in Europe where the Field Vole or closely allied races do not occur, and throughout Great Britain and many of its islands the species is abundant wherever there is sufficient grassland to suit its habits.

In the Orkneys its place is taken by the large Orkney Vole, but the common form, or at least closely related forms, inhabit many of the Hebridean Islands. It is not known in Ireland.

Sociable in its habits, colonies, often consisting of a large number of individuals, are generally to be found among the rough pasturage of meadows or sheep-walks, especially in luxuriant moist localities, as this species is fond of water. In such places their runs may be seen spreading in all directions, either winding among the herbage or tunnelled under the surface of the ground.

From the earliest times in history attention has been directed to the destruction caused to crops and pasturage by these animals, when favourable conditions have caused their numbers to increase beyond normal bounds, and what is known as a 'Vole plague' or a 'Vole year' occurs.

In such circumstances the animals swarm in masses over agricultural lands like a scourge of locusts, eating every green blade and barking the stems of young trees.

On these occasions, it has usually been noticed how speedily this concentration of animal life attracts the attention of various birds and beasts of prey, such as Owls, Kestrels, Weasels, and Foxes, who decimate the hordes, but hardly account for the sudden disappearance of the plague, which generally happens from natural causes. These are chiefly the failure of the food supply when the fields are eaten bare, and consequent weakness and disease.

In Great Britain 'Vole years' are comparatively rare, but from 1891 to 1893 a great increase of the species occurred in the border lands of Scotland, where many miles of grassland were devastated.

A succession of mild winters seems to be a contributory cause in the abnormal increase of this species, while hard

continued on page 74

Pl. 31.

Field-Vole.

Bank Vole.
Orkney Vole.

continued from Plate 31

The Common Field Vole

winters with severe frosts help to keep their numbers within bounds.

The Field Vole breeds three or four times in the season, producing from two or three to nine young at a time.

The nest is made of grasses and placed either on the surface or in a hole underground, the situation depending on the time of year. Mr Millais observed a pair making their nursery and was struck with the rapidity with which they carried out the work.

In the part of Surrey with which I am best acquainted, I find the Field Vole – sometimes called the 'Old Sheep-dog Mouse' from its short tail – to be generally less abundant than the Bank Vole, whose numbers seem less liable to fluctuation, and, owing to the almost exclusively vegetarian tastes of the former, it is seldom tempted by the ordinary bait in mousetraps.

Its favourite food consists of the juicy stems of grasses, but young shoots of heather and various other plants are eaten.

The Field Vole soon becomes tame in captivity, and unlike mice and most other rodents seldom attempts to bite when handled.

The Orkney Vole
Microtus orcadensis, Millais
pl. 31 **bottom right**

This fine Vole, whose discovery as a distinct species we owe to Mr Millais, was first described by him in the *Zoologist* (July 1904), though he had observed its distinctive features some years previously.

The maximum size of the species, given by this naturalist in his *Mammals of Great Britain and Ireland*, is: head and body 140 millimetres (5½ inches), tail 30 millimetres (1 3/16 inches), the dimensions in very large males being nearly double those of the Common Field Vole.

Some living specimens in Autumn pelage I had an opportunity of examining were in colour a yellowish brown above, with underparts of a yellowish buff. Compared with the mainland Vole, this island species has a rounder head and much blunter muzzle and also a more bushy growth of the fur on the cheeks.

Superficially it has a good deal of resemblance to the Water Vole, but according to Mr Millais it is more closely related to the Common Field Vole. The majority of the specimens first obtained were from Pomona, the main island of the Orkneys, but the species has been found inhabiting all the larger islands of the group, except Hoy.

It frequents the grass and clover fields on the lower parts of the islands and prefers moist localities. Black varieties of the species are not uncommon.

Plate 32

Sub-Genus ARVICOLA

The Water Vole
Arvicola amphibius, Linnaeus
pl. 32

The Water Vole, often called the Water Rat, is the largest of its family, the adults usually measuring about 8½ inches in length of head and body and about 4½ inches in length of tail, though a good deal of variation occurs in the size of different specimens. The form is characterised by its general stoutness, and the tail is proportionally longer than in the other Voles. The ears are short, and sometimes nearly concealed by the long bushy fur.

In colour, the glossy upper parts are greyish brown, often tinged with russet; the underparts are somewhat lighter.

A black variety, first described by MacGillivray, often occurs, chiefly in the more northern parts of Scotland, but also in England, especially in the fen districts of Cambridgeshire and Norfolk. Although sub-specific rank has lately been given to this race, the only difference appears to be in the darker colour and rather smaller size. A figure of one is shown in the background of the Plate.

The Water Vole inhabits the greater part of Europe, and is also well distributed over Northern Asia.

It is abundant in places suited to its amphibious tastes over most of England and Scotland, but, like the others of this family, is unknown in Ireland.

Haunting the banks of quiet, weedy streams, ponds, or wide ditches, it is seldom found far from water.

As usual in many of our small rodents it appears to be short-sighted, and consequently may be watched at very close quarters if the observer will only remain still. Under these conditions it is interesting to study its habits. It likes to leave its hiding place in the daytime, when it may often be seen sitting up on its haunches busily brushing and cleansing its coat or engaged in a meal. In habits it is almost entirely vegetarian, chiefly eating the shoots, leaves, and roots of different water plants and also the bark of trees. Turnips and potatoes are sometimes attacked in winter, and acorns too are eaten at this time.

The Water Vole has been accused of taking fish, but if it does so this is not a common habit. As the Common Brown Rat often resorts to the banks of streams for a living, it is not unlikely that the two species are sometimes confused.

If disturbed when sitting by a stream, the Water Vole instantly dives, and swimming under water seeks the entrance of his burrow, which is often below the surface, but there is usually a second outlet leading to the air. When in danger and requiring at the same time to come to the surface to breathe, the Water Vole will cleverly conceal its whereabouts by rising under the cover of floating vegetation or some such protection.

In shallow water one can generally follow with the eye the direction taken, by the cloudy track of mud disturbed by the action of the animal.

A nest of dry grass and other herbage is made for the young either in a burrow or above ground among protecting vegetation, where from four to five are born at a time.

Pl.32.

Water Vole. 2/3

Plate 33

Group or Sub-Order DUPLICIDENTATA
Family LEPORIDAE Genus LEPUS

The Common Hare

Lepus europaeus, Pallas
pl. 33

This species, the largest of British rodents, measures in length of head and body about 22 inches, the tail 3¼ inches, and the ears about 4¾ inches; the weight of the animal being from 7 to 10 pounds.

The general colour of the fur is a tawny buff, irregularly broken with darker tints where the blackish underparts of the hairs come into view and relieve the yellow tips.

This want of uniformity in the colour is caused by the peculiar character of the fur, which curls and twists in various directions, especially along the back and upper parts of the animal, where it is thickest.

The neck and shoulders and also the legs are more of a pure yellowish buff. The underparts of the body and tail are pure white, the latter being black on its upper surface.

The ears are a mixture of brown and buff, nearly white behind, and with black tips. In the winter coat the colour is more inclined to grey.

The large and prominent yellowish eyes are so placed that the animal has a good view of anything behind, but sees indistinctly straight ahead.

The hind feet and legs are very strong, and greatly exceed the fore legs in length.

If one examines the tracks of a running Hare or Rabbit in the snow, it will be seen that the hind feet touch the surface well in front of the fore feet, owing to the forward swing of the former when the animal is moving fast.

From ancient times the Hare has always been considered as one of the animals which chew the cud, but the late Mr Robert Drane of Cardiff, who made a close study of this species in captivity, states (*Trans. Cardiff Naturalists' Society*, vol. xxvii, part ii. 1894–95) that his 'own belief is that not only does the Hare never chew the cud, but that he cannot. The Hare has a habit when at rest, as when sitting in its form, of grinding its teeth, probably to keep them in order. May not this be the origin of the assumption that it is chewing the cud?' According to this authority, the food is passed a second time through the body.

The Common Hare is widely distributed over Europe as far north as Scandinavia and Northern Russia and eastwards to the Caucasus. In Great Britain, where it is said to differ slightly from the Continental form, it is plentiful about cultivated ground, especially grasslands, when not driven away by the persecution of man.

This species, though not a native of Ireland, has been introduced there at different times.

It has also been established in the Shetlands, Orkneys and some of the Western Isles of Scotland.

Before the passing of the Ground Game Act in 1880, Hares appear everywhere to have been much more numerous than they are today.

As a rule they prefer the lower cultivated lands and grassy downs, but they will often ascend the higher hills, as in Perthshire, where according to Mr Millais, he has frequently seen and shot them at an altitude of about 1500 feet above Pitlochry.

Except in the breeding season, Hares are usually unsociable in habits, differing in this and in many other ways from Rabbits.

They make no underground burrow, their shelter known as a 'form' being merely a lair to rest in during the daytime, generally situated in the shade in summer or in some sunny spot in winter.

Trusting to their protective colouring, Hares will often sit so tight in their hiding place that they may be almost trodden on.

Towards evening they come forth to feed on the grasses, clover, young corn and the various kinds of herbs which make up their diet. Carrots, turnips, and other vegetables growing in fields and gardens are also attacked, and often in hard winters the bark of young trees is eaten.

The speed at which this animal can travel when hard pressed is astonishing, its highest having been estimated at some thirty miles an hour. If chased it generally runs uphill to gain the benefit of the long hind legs.

The Hare is a good swimmer and will cross wide rivers to get access to some favourite feeding ground or to escape an enemy.

In one of the severe winters about 1880 I once observed a Hare, when chased by a Collie dog, boldly enter the freezing water of the River Tweed. After crossing, at full speed, a broad stretch of ice along the banks, it plunged in where the current kept the water partly clear from ice and where the dog was afraid to follow. Crossing the stream the Hare attempted without success to climb the ice on the farther side, but after struggling for a time, was compelled to return, and I was unable to see what eventually happened as it made for a point lower down the river where it was lost to view.

The Hare produces from two to five young at a time and may breed at any time of the year, though February and March are the usual courting months, when the bucks fight savagely for possession of the does.

The leverets, unlike the young of the Rabbit which are born naked and blind, are well clothed with fur and can see just after birth.

As soon as her family arrives, the mother separates her young, placing them apart in different hiding places where she can visit and suckle them at night.

The Hare has always been highly esteemed for purposes of sport, and in former days was reckoned among the 'five wild beasts of venery', namely the Hart, the Hind, the Hare, the Boar, and the Wolf.

At one time special sanctuaries appear to have been set apart to encourage the increase and give protection to the Hare. One of these is still in existence near Cheam, Surrey, which is said to date from Tudor times.

My friend Col Godwin Austin tells me he remembers another still in use in his younger days but now demolished, situated on the top of Merrow Down, Guildford. These sanctuaries consisted of enclosures of several acres encircled by high walls, with convenient holes for the going out and coming in of the animals.

Besides their cry of pain when in distress, Hares have softer notes, used when calling each other or when the mother is suckling her young.

Common Hare ⅓

Plate 34

The Mountain Hare
Lepus timidus, Linnaeus
pl. 34 **left** (autumn)

The Mountain Hare, the *Lepus variabilis* of Pallas, often known as the Alpine, White, Blue, or Varying Hare, is smaller and in general has more the character of the Rabbit than our Common Brown Hare.

The head is rounder, the ears and tail relatively shorter, and the fur thicker and more woolly in texture. In length the head and body measure about 21½ inches, the tail 2½ inches, and the ears about 3¼ inches. The average weight may be put at 5 or 6 pounds.

In summer the coat is a dusky yellowish brown in colour, changing as the season advances to a bluish grey before assuming the pure white of the full winter pelage.

The underparts and greater portion of the tail are at all times white, while the tips of the ears are always black.

When changing colour these Hares often acquire a patchy or piebald appearance and are then very conspicuous. From the observations of MacGillivray and others, the chief annual moult takes place in spring, but a more or less slight and irregular renewal of the coat may occur at other times of the year. The change of colour generally begins in September, when the brown of summer turns to bluish grey, and gradually bleaching, usually attains its pure winter whiteness by December. Often however some brown remains about the head and ears, while the back is grizzled with darker hairs, as shown in Plate 35. Individuals also differ considerably when renewing their summer coat and frequently retain a good deal of their winter colouring till April.

This species inhabits the northern as well as the mountainous parts of Europe and is also widely distributed in the Arctic regions. A closely related species takes its place in North America.

In the British Islands the chief headquarters of the Mountain Hare are in the Highlands of northern and central Scotland. At one time it appears to have inhabited the Orkneys, though now extinct there, but it exists on some of the Hebridean Islands, where it has been introduced at various times. Its range has lately been extended in many parts of southern and southwestern Scotland, mainly by introduction. In Midlothian, it is found on the Pentlands and Moorfoots, among the Lammermuirs in Berwickshire and on the hilly parts of Peeblesshire, Selkirkshire, Lanarkshire, and Ayrshire.

The Mountain Hare has also been established in some parts of England and Wales. In Ireland it is represented by a sub-species, the Irish Hare.

In character the Mountain Hare differs in many ways from its cousin of the lowlands, being less suspicious and in consequence more easily approached. It shows some affinity to the Rabbit in taking cover from its enemies in holes among the peat or in hiding places under broken rocks.

When undisturbed it may be seen moving to and fro along the slopes of the hills or sitting quietly in the shelter of some rock or peat hag, often looking very conspicuous against dark surroundings in its white winter coat.

When disturbed this species always runs uphill if possible, moving fast at first but soon slackening its pace; at a distance of some sixty or seventy yards it invariably stops and looks around to reconnoitre before proceeding on its course. These manoeuvres are carried on till the animal passes out of sight. The best time to study the Mountain Hare at close quarters is during the breeding season in April, when they may be seen running about in all directions and are at the same time comparatively tame.

Three, four, or five leverets are born at a time, which like those of the Common Hare, are already clothed with hair at birth. The food consists chiefly of grasses and heather and also at times of moss and lichen.

Apart from man, its chief enemies are the Hill Fox and Golden Eagle who kill large numbers, the latter especially being very destructive.

The Mountain Hare does not always keep to his hilly fastnesses, but will often come down to the lower ground in hard weather and occasionally at other times. When it meets the Brown Hare on the lower levels the two species will interbreed.

The Irish Hare
Lepus timidus hibernicus, Yarrell
pl. 34 **right**

The Irish Hare closely resembles the Mountain Hare of Scotland and is considered as only a sub-species or variety by Mr Millais, but the late Major Barrett-Hamilton gives it full specific rank.

The Irish Hare differs from the other chiefly in its greater size and weight, and more distinct reddish-brown colour. Owing to the milder climate of Ireland it is also less subject to the usual whitening process in the winter coat, which often retains its darker hue.

This question of seasonal colour was formerly thought to be the chief point of difference between the two animals, but it is now known that the Irish Hare often turns partially and sometimes wholly white in winter, even in specimens introduced into England. A not uncommon buff variety of this Hare is found along the coast of County Dublin and in other parts of Ireland. This variety is also sometimes met with in the Island of Mull, Scotland, where Irish Hares were imported many years ago. Millais says, 'In Mull the Hares of Irish blood are fairly numerous; they are larger than the Scotch ones and unlike their cousins *do not become white* in winter.'

The Irish Hare is not confined to the mountainous districts of its native country, but occurs also on the low grounds, and in habits does not appear to differ in any way from the Mountain Hares of Scotland.

Pl. 34.

Mountain Hare. (autumn)

Irish Hare.

Plate 35

The Mountain Hare
Lepus timidus, Linnaeus
pl. 35 (winter)

The Mountain Hare, the *Lepus variabilis* of Pallas, often known as the Alpine, White, Blue, or Varying Hare, is smaller and in general has more the character of the Rabbit than our Common Brown Hare.

The head is rounder, the ears and tail relatively shorter, and the fur thicker and more woolly in texture. In length the head and body measure about 21½ inches, the tail 2½ inches, and the ears about 3¼ inches. The average weight may be put at 5 or 6 pounds.

In summer the coat is a dusky yellowish brown in colour, changing as the season advances to a bluish grey before assuming the pure white of the full winter pelage.

The underparts and greater portion of the tail are at all times white, while the tips of the ears are always black.

When changing colour these Hares often acquire a patchy or piebald appearance and are then very conspicuous. From the observations of MacGillivray and others, the chief annual moult takes place in spring, but a more or less slight and irregular renewal of the coat may occur at other times of the year. The change of colour generally begins in September, when the brown of summer turns to bluish grey, and gradually bleaching, usually attains its pure winter whiteness by December. Often however some brown remains about the head and ears, while the back is grizzled with darker hairs, as shown in Plate 35. Individuals also differ considerably when renewing their summer coat and frequently retain a good deal of their winter colouring till April.

This species inhabits the northern as well as the mountainous parts of Europe and is also widely distributed in the Arctic regions. A closely related species takes its place in North America.

In the British Islands the chief headquarters of the Mountain Hare are in the Highlands of northern and central Scotland. At one time it appears to have inhabited the Orkneys, though now extinct there, but it exists on some of the Hebridean Islands, where it has been introduced at various times. Its range has lately been extended in many parts of southern and south-western Scotland, mainly by introduction. In Midlothian, it is found on the Pentlands and Moorfoots, among the Lammermuirs in Berwickshire and on the hilly parts of Peeblesshire, Selkirkshire, Lanarkshire, and Ayrshire.

The Mountain Hare has also been established in some parts of England and Wales. In Ireland it is represented by a sub-species, the Irish Hare.

In character the Mountain Hare differs in many ways from its cousin of the lowlands, being less suspicious and in consequence more easily approached. It shows some affinity to the Rabbit in taking cover from its enemies in holes among the peat or in hiding places under broken rocks.

When undisturbed it may be seen moving to and fro along the slopes of the hills or sitting quietly in the shelter of some rock or peat hag, often looking very conspicuous against dark surroundings in its white winter coat.

When disturbed this species always runs uphill if possible, moving fast at first but soon slackening its pace; at a distance of some sixty or seventy yards it invariably stops and looks around to reconnoitre before proceeding on its course. These manoeuvres are carried on till the animal passes out of sight. The best time to study the Mountain Hare at close quarters is during the breeding season in April, when they may be seen running about in all directions and are at the same time comparatively tame.

Three, four, or five leverets are born at a time, which, like those of the Common Hare, are already clothed with hair at birth. The food consists chiefly of grasses and heather and also at times of moss and lichen.

Apart from man, its chief enemies are the Hill Fox and Golden Eagle who kill large numbers, the latter especially being very destructive.

The Mountain Hare does not always keep to his hilly fastnesses, but will often come down to the lower ground in hard weather and occasionally at other times. When it meets the Brown Hare on the lower levels the two species will interbreed.

Pl. 35.

Mountain Hare. (winter)

Plate 36

The Rabbit or Cony
Lepus cuniculus
pl. 36

Compared with the Common Hare, the Rabbit is considerably smaller, the head and body are relatively of stouter build and the ears and legs shorter. The fur is also of a softer texture. The total length from nose to root of tail is about 17 inches, the ears 3½ inches.

The predominating colour of the fur is a grizzled greyish brown, the nape of the neck reddish buff, the underparts of the body and tail pure white. The margins of the ears are dark, and show no black tips as in those of the Hare.

Blaine, in his *Encyclopaedia of Rural Sports* (1875), appears to have been the first to draw attention to the more massive head of the buck Rabbit, compared with the slimmer one of the doe.

The weight of a full grown animal is about 3 pounds.

In history the earliest accounts of this species refer to its abundance in Spain and Portugal, as well as in Corsica and the Balearic Islands, where we are told ferrets were used for its capture much as they are today. It is also found in the Azores, Madeira, and the Canaries, where it is said to be indigenous.

From the Iberian Peninsula it appears to have spread to France and other parts of the continent of Europe.

According to Barrett-Hamilton (*A History of British Mammals*, p. 184) the supposition that the Rabbit was introduced into Britain by the Romans is without foundation, 'as it had no native name in any part of these Kingdoms until the Normans came over and named it.'

Dr Browne, writing in his *Life of Bede*, describes one of the robes – presumably made between 1085 and 1104 – and used when the body of St Cuthbert was removed from Lindisfarne to Durham, as having pictured on the border of the garment a horseman 'with hawk in hand and a row of rabbits below'.

When once introduced it seems to have spread rapidly in England, where it was valued on account of its skin as well as the flesh. In Scotland it appears to have been at first chiefly confined to the eastern lowlands and some of the islands, and it was long before it reached the Highlands.

According to Mr J. H. Dixon in his account of the parish of Gairloch, Ross-shire, the Rabbit was quite unknown there till about 1850, when it was introduced at Letterewe. Now it is abundant in all suitable parts of the county.

It is also plentiful in Ireland, where it was brought in in early times.

Rabbits are very sociable in their habits, usually living in colonies, and making comfortable homes for themselves in dark underground burrows, which are often very elaborate in their construction, and are used as a safe retreat during the day. As evening approaches the occupants come out to feed, or to frolic and play, when a Rabbit warren presents a busy scene.

Light sandy soil with plenty of cover is best suited to the habits of this species, but they may be found inhabiting almost any ground not too damp and exposed. In the Highlands of Scotland they usually make their retreats under the shelter of rocks.

The excellence of the turf in Rabbit warrens, owing to the close cropping of the various grasses, is well known. Furze also forms a favourite food, and along the shores of the Moray Firth and elsewhere the bushes of this plant are so constantly trimmed by the animals' teeth that they assume curious shapes, and often look like footstools.

There are few garden flowers or shrubs which escape the Rabbit's attention, especially when freshly planted, as anything newly put in seems always to tempt his appetite.

Mr J. E. Harting, in his account of the Rabbit ('Fur and Feather Series,' p. 6), refers to the difference in the manner of attacking turnips shown by this species compared with the Hare. The latter 'will bite off the peel and leave it on the ground; a rabbit will eat peel and all'.

When preparing her nursery, the doe generally seeks some situation far removed from the rest of the community. Here she excavates a burrow running several feet under ground, and at the farthest end makes a nest of dry bents or similar material, and lines it with fur from her own belly. From five to eight or nine naked and blind young are born at a time.

They are visited and fed by the mother at night, who carefully closes the entrance of the 'stop' or burrow before leaving them in the early morning.

I have seen a doe in broad daylight on a summer morning stealing quietly away from the neighbourhood of her burrow, which she had made in a flower bed not far from my window.

Occasionally Rabbits have been known to produce their young in a nest or form on the ground, after the manner of a Hare.

As a rule the Rabbit is a silent animal, though it will scream loudly when in pain or fear. When suspicious of danger or alarmed they have a way of stamping loudly with their hind feet as a warning to their neighbours, and also make use of their white tails as a danger signal.

When travelling to and fro Rabbits keep to favourite tracks or runs among grass and herbage, and, if these beaten paths are closely examined, they will show that the footsteps are placed at regular intervals and always more or less on the same spot. This habit is well known to rabbit catchers when setting their snares.

Rabbits have many natural enemies, and chiefly suffer from the attacks of the Fox and Stoat and some of the larger birds of prey.

The so-called Belgian Hare is only a large form of the domestic Rabbit, as the Hare and Rabbit have never been known to interbreed.

Pl.36

Rabbit. ⅓.

Plate 37

Order RUMINANTIA
Family CERVIDAE Sub-Family CERVINAE Genus CERVUS

The Red Deer
Cervus elaphus, Linnaeus
pl. 37

This typical species is unquestionably the grandest wild animal we now possess in the British Islands. Like the rest of its family the Red Deer is characterised by the branching antlers peculiar to the male only in all species except the Reindeer, where they are present in both sexes. They are shed every year, and speedily replaced by an entirely new growth. Another distinguishing character in this group is the spotted coat of the young, which in some species is retained by the adults.

The Red Deer or Stag measures about 4 feet high at the withers, and about 6 feet from nose to end of tail, but different examples vary a good deal in size. The colour in summer is reddish brown, greyer on the face and throat, and with a distinct yellowish patch, edged with black, on the hind quarters.

In late autumn and winter the coat is longer and thicker, especially about the neck, and the colour changes to a greyer brown, which often takes a darker hue from contact with peaty ground, where the animal has 'soiled'.

The pale clay-coloured eye gives the Stag a curious sinister expression when excited. Below the eye is a cavity known as the 'tear-pit', containing a yellow waxy secretion.

The antlers are rounded, and when fully developed each usually branches into three 'tines' pointing forwards, with three more points at the top starting from a cup-like depression, but great variation occurs in the number and shape of the points as well as in the size of the horns.

In the first year of a Stag's life the growth consists of a single pair of spikes, in the next the brow points are developed, and afterwards the points increase in number till in his sixth year he is usually fully grown, and often has a head of twelve points, when he is known as a 'Royal'.

According to Millais, wild Stags in England shed their horns in April, those in Scotland a month later.

Good shelter and abundance of suitable food increase the size and number of points in the antlers, as surely as less favourable conditions, such as poor feeding and overcrowding, cause deterioration.

There are no wild Deer in the British Islands today approaching in any way the great Stags which inhabited our forests far back in prehistoric times, whose wonderful antlers of many points and enormous beam are occasionally dug out of peat deposits or river beds, and dwarf by comparison our best Scottish specimens of modern times.

When the Red Stag casts his horns in spring, the new growth, which increases rapidly, is at first soft, very sensitive, and clothed in a delicate hairy covering known as 'velvet'. When the new horn is complete, this outer covering dries, and as it peels is removed by the action of the animal, who may be seen at this time rubbing his horns against rocks, banks of peat, or trees.

The Red Deer is found inhabiting forest country throughout the greater part of Europe, ranging as far north as Norway, Sweden, and Russia, and southwards to Corsica and Sardinia, but it is now unknown in Greece and Italy.

It also inhabits Asia Minor and North Africa. This species is indigenous in the British Islands, where in prehistoric times and for long afterwards it was abundant in the vast forests covering the face of the land.

The chase of the Stag formed one of the favourite pastimes of the Norman Kings and their followers, who reserved large tracts of country in which they could indulge in the sport, and where the Deer and other wild animals were protected under the cruel forest law.

A few Red Deer still linger in the New Forest, and many more among the moors and woodlands of North Devon and Somerset. Some also remain in Westmorland, besides numerous herds living under semi-feral conditions, or in parks. According to Mr Millais (*Mammals of Great Britain and Ireland*, vol. iii. p. 109), thirty-one parks and more than seventy hays (small enclosures) are mentioned in Domesday Book as existing at the time, and of these only one remains today, namely, Eridge Park (Reredfelle) in Sussex, the property of Lord Abergavenny.

In Scotland, north of the Forth and Clyde, deer forests are numerous, the land under deer having increased enormously since the beginning of the nineteenth century, until at one time the territory given over to these animals stretched almost from sea to sea across parts of northern Scotland.

Since the late war, however, much of this wild country has been utilized for the grazing of sheep.

To those who have been privileged to watch the Red Deer among the glens and hills of Scotland, or to hear his wild and far-reaching notes of defiance as he challenges some rival, nothing else would seem to fit in so well with the spirit of his surroundings as this fine animal, whose form is a model of strength and elegance.

One wonders at his stoutness of heart and untiring muscles as he breasts some hill without a pause with his long swinging stride.

The breeding season begins in October, and after this the sexes separate and keep more or less apart till the following autumn.

Though grass is their principal food, they are fond of the leaves of trees, and do a great deal of damage to crops when near their haunts. A well-known habit of the Red Deer is its partiality for chewing bones and cast-off antlers, which are often found gnawed and worn by the teeth of the animal.

Though timid and shy of human beings when in a wild condition, few animals are more dangerous than a Stag which has become sufficiently tame to lose his fear of man, as sometimes happens in the rutting season, when fatal accidents have often happened. Even wild Stags when they have taken to plantations near houses, as they sometimes do, and in consequence have lost some of their natural shyness, are not always to be trusted.

The hind brings forth her single calf early in summer, and for some time keeps it hidden in a bed of bracken or other thick cover. The young are marked with spots of white on the back and sides, which are retained till the following spring.

According to Millais, wild Stags do not reach their prime till they are eleven years of age, and remain at their best for another four or five years.

84

Pl. 37.

Red Deer.

Plate 38

The Fallow Deer
Cervus dama, Linnaeus
pl. 38

Standing 3 feet high at the shoulders and measuring from nose to tip of the tail about 5 feet 8 inches, this species differs considerably in form and character from the Red Deer.

The horns of the Fallow Deer have two anterior tines in each, and have no 'bay' tine. The upper part of the beam is flattened out like the palm of a hand, and broken up on the top and behind into several spikes of various length, the lowest, known as the back point, being the longest and most distinct in normal heads.

In many of the New Forest bucks the form of antler differs from that of the ordinary Fallow Deer in parks, and resembles the type found among some of the wild species in Asia, whose horns are much less palmated and more broken up with prongs.

In summer coat, the colour of the Fallow Deer is as a rule of a yellowish russet on the upper parts of the body, boldly spotted with white, with a stripe of the same colour extending along the flanks. The under side of the tail and surrounding parts are conspicuously white, and the belly and inner sides of the legs are also light.

In winter the white spots disappear, and the colour of the body darkens to a greyer brown. This description applies only to the typical Fallow Deer, but in most parks where deer have lived for generations in a semi-domestic condition, various varieties are found, from an almost uniform black hue to pure white. These aberrations in colour are not of recent occurrence, but have been known in England for several centuries, even before King James I brought into Scotland the dark race of this Deer.

The Fallow Deer appears to be a native in most of the countries bordering the Mediterranean, including the island of Sardinia, and has been introduced as a park animal into many other parts of Europe. It also occurs in Western Asia and until recently in North Africa.

When or by whom the species was first introduced to the British Islands remains a mystery, but it was probably imported by the Romans during their occupation of the country or by some early traders.

It was certainly plentiful soon after the Norman Conquest, as we know by the writings of the chroniclers.

Chiefly for sporting purposes, herds of Fallow and Red Deer were in early times kept in parks, where they were either hunted with hounds or driven by beaters near enough to the sportsmen of those days to be shot with the bow and arrow. This appears to have been a favourite amusement of Queen Elizabeth and other sovereigns.

Now the park Fallow Deer is usually kept as an ornament, but a remnant of the old stock still inhabit the New Forest and other ancient hunting grounds.

As we see them in parks, Fallow Deer generally associate in herds, and like the Red Deer, the sexes keep apart during a great part of the year. According to Millais, the bucks shed their horns in May and have them renewed and free from velvet in August.

The rutting season begins in October, when the grunting notes of the male are heard and combats take place for possession of the does. Fatal wounds are seldom received in these encounters, as the thrust of a Fallow buck's horn is less deadly than that of the Red Stag, though I have seen a buck which had recently lost his eye.

The doe usually gives birth to a single fawn in the month of June or occasionally at a later time in summer.

In common with other deer, this species likes to browse on the leaves of trees.

The extinct Giant Fallow Deer (*Cervus megaceros*) whose bones have been found in various parts of the British Islands, but chiefly in the peatbogs of Ireland, was a magnificent animal standing some 6 or 7 feet high at the withers and possessing great palmated horns weighing up to 100 pounds, and with a span of about 10 feet.

PL. 38

Fallow Deer. ♂

Plate 39

Genus CAPREOLUS

The Roe Deer
Capreolus capreolus, Linnaeus
pl. 39

Much smaller than either of the preceding species, the Roe stands about 26 inches high at the shoulders, and measures 4 feet from nose to tail.

A full grown buck may weigh over 60 pounds, but the average weight is less.

The striking change in the colour and texture of the coat as the season advances is remarkable. Between May and September or October, the body is lightly clothed with hair of a bright chestnut red, with a white patch on the rump and the muzzle beautifully marked with black and white, as shown in the Plate.

In winter, when the coat becomes very thick and long, it changes to a dark greyish brown or mouse-colour, and the throat is marked with two light patches. The tail is almost concealed by the long hair of the rump.

The Roe buck's horns first appear in his second year as single prongs, in the next season's growth the brow tines are developed, which in turn are succeeded by the complete antlers, each having a brow and two top points. This is the normal head of the roe, but examples occur with a larger number of points, especially in the forests of Germany. The horns are generally cast in November and are renewed and free from velvet by the following April.

An interesting observation has been made by Mr Millais, that the Roe of Pleistocene times, whose horns are found from time to time in our forest-beds and brick-earth, are, with few exceptions, in no way superior to good modern Scottish heads, while the prehistoric remains of the Red Deer show how vastly superior these animals must have been, compared with those of today.

Good Roe horns measure about 9½ inches.

This species inhabits the greater part of Europe, ranging as far north as Sweden and southwards to Italy and Greece. It is also a native of Asia Minor and Northern Asia. Larger forms are found eastwards in Siberia and in the mountains of Manchuria. The Roe was formerly abundant throughout the greater part of England, where it was reckoned among the beasts of chase, but the original stock appears gradually to have become extinct, with the exception of a few which lingered in the northern counties.

They have since been introduced into various parts of the country and now exist in the New Forest, Dorsetshire, Sussex, Epping Forest, Cumberland and Northumberland. Roe are not uncommon in the neighbourhood of Godalming, Surrey, where they run wild among the surrounding woodlands. I have seen them on several occasions and even noticed their footprints in my garden. These deer probably strayed at some time from Petworth or Virginia Water.

The Roe has been known from the earliest times in Scotland, and still exists there in large numbers in the northern woods and glens. Their chief stronghold seems to be in Perthshire, and the country about Forres and Beauly, though they are also numerous in many other parts, wherever they can find large tracts of timber with thick undergrowth.

Though the Roe is not indigenous in Ireland some have been introduced there.

These graceful creatures are seldom found far from woods, though they will often leave the seclusion of their cover and come out to the heather of the open moorland in summer. Browsing early in the morning and again in the evening or at night, they pass the greater part of the day hiding in the cover of bracken, brambles, or some other similar protection.

As their sense of smell and hearing, as well as their eyesight, is very acute, they are difficult to see until disturbed, when the conspicuous white patch on their hinder parts is very distinct as they dash aside through the undergrowth.

The Roe is much less sociable in its habits than the Red or Fallow Deer, and is often found alone or in pairs, though many individuals may be scattered about in a favourite stretch of woodland.

Leaves of all kinds, especially those of the bramble and ivy, tender shoots of trees and also berries are all favourite food of the Roe. It does a good deal of harm sometimes by nibbling the bark of trees, and in Surrey I have had a small apple tree destroyed in this way.

The sexes pair in July and remain in company until the early part of August.

The strange phenomenon in the life history of the Roe, namely, that little apparent development of the unborn young takes place until December, in which month the growth becomes normal, was first investigated by Professor Bischoff and later by Franz Keibel, who have shown that gestation lasts for forty weeks.

At the end of May or beginning of June the doe gives birth to her two fawns, which in colour are dark brown, spotted with yellowish white. The young are early trained by the mother to squat close to the ground and lie hidden in the presence of danger.

The curious circular tracks or runs trodden in the grass by this species in the woods near Cawdor Castle have been described by Mr Millais in his *British Deer and their Horns*. These rings are caused by the constant treading of the animals, as they chase each other when playing among the trees and herbage.

Plate 40

Family BOVIDAE Genus BOS

Wild White Cattle
Bos taurus, Linnaeus
pl. 40

It is difficult to trace with any certainty the origin of the so-called 'Wild' Cattle living under semi-feral conditions today, and now considered by most authorities to be descended in all probability from domestic animals which had escaped from captivity at some remote period, and after sheltering for an unknown time in our forests as truly wild creatures, were driven into enclosures in medieval times.

It is therefore a question whether they should be included in a work of this kind, but as the history of the different breeds is of some interest a short account of the principal herds is given.

Mr Millais considers (*Mammals of Great Britain and Ireland,* vol. iii. p. 188) that 'there is a strong probability that the 'Wild' Cattle and all our domestic cattle are descended from breeds produced on the Continent, and that these, after centuries of domestication elsewhere, were introduced into Britain. As far as we can guess, these breeds originally came from the Urus, but at so remote a date that the very earliest history and pictures can give no clue.'

An early domesticated Ox, known as *Bos longifrons,* whose bones have been found in large numbers along with the flint implements of ancient Britons, is said to be the origin of our small Welsh and Highland Cattle.

Though Darwin and other naturalists considered our Park Cattle to be most likely directly descended from the Urus, Professor Owen, Dr J. A. Smith, E. R. Alston and others do not hold this view, but look upon them as originally a domestic breed, whose wildness has been partly due to their environment.

According to Mr Harting (*Extinct British Animals,* p. 220) White Cattle *with red ears* are referred to in the Welsh laws of Howell Dha about A.D. 940 and Wild Cattle are mentioned in the forest laws of King Canute (A.D. 1014–35).

Again they are included among other wild beasts inhabiting the great forests around London by Fitz-Stephen about 1174. In the great Caledonian woods of Central Scotland, pure white forest bulls, with manes like lions, are described by Hector Boece, which may possibly have been the ancestors of the herd which at one time existed at Blair Athole.

As the land became more settled and the forests began to disappear, what were left of the cattle in various parts of Britain were driven into enclosures belonging to the great landed proprietors, where they still remain in one or two localities at the present day.

Perhaps the best known and most famous of the remaining herds is the one at Chillingham Castle, Northumberland, owned by the Earl of Tankerville, where the park extends to about 1100 acres. This enclosure is referred to as far back as 1292 as containing wild animals, apparently those which had been driven in from the surrounding district.

In Plate 41 I have shown the head of a Chillingham Bull drawn from life.

In this breed the horns turn upwards and inwards, the inside of the ears and upper part of the muzzle are reddish brown, and the rest of the animal creamy white.

In Mr Storer's *Wild White Cattle of Great Britain,* pp. 156–157, is given an interesting account of the habits of the Chillingham herd by the late Lord Tankerville, from which the following is quoted: 'They have, in the first place, pre-eminently all the characteristics of wild animals, with some peculiarities that are sometimes very curious and amusing.

'They hide their young and feed in the night, basking or sleeping during the day.

'They are fierce when pressed, but generally speaking very timorous, moving off on the appearance of anyone even at a great distance; yet this varies very much in different seasons of the year, and according to the manner in which they are approached. In summer I have been for several weeks at a time without getting a sight of them – they, on the slightest appearance of anyone, retiring into a wood which serves them as a sanctuary. . . .

'It is observable of them, as of red deer, that they have a peculiar faculty of taking advantage of the irregularities of the ground, so that on being disturbed they may traverse the whole park, and yet you hardly get a sight of them.'

The Chillingham Cattle have not always been distinguished by their reddish-brown ears, as in 1692 the majority are said to have been black-eared, and when Bewick wrote, a few of this type still existed.

Cadzow Castle, Lanarkshire, owned by the Duke of Hamilton, has another fine herd of White Cattle in the park including part of the ancient Caledonian Forest. This forest was formerly used as a hunting ground by the Scottish kings and still retained many of its fine old trees when I saw it some years ago.

In this breed the animals have black ears and muzzle, the legs and feet are spotted with the same colour and the horns are rather more spreading than those of the Chillingham herd.

They show a good many wild traits in their habits and are dangerous if approached too closely.

Their appearance is very striking when seen among their wild surroundings of natural forest.

A bull and cow of the breed are shown on Plate 40.

Chartley Park, Staffordshire, was the home of an ancient herd of White Cattle until 1905. I am indebted to the Duke of Bedford for kindly supplying me with the following particulars of this interesting breed at the present time (January 21st, 1921): 'The Chartley Herd (at Woburn). Owner, The Duke of Bedford, K.G., Woburn Abbey, Bedfordshire. This herd is said to have been driven into Chartley Park from the royal forest of Needwood in the reign of Henry III, where they remained until May 1905, when they were bought by the Duke of Bedford. At that time they only numbered seven, and unfortunately they died without leaving any pure bred progeny. Finding that there was no hope of saving the pure bred stock, their new owner crossed a bull with Longhorn cows. This experiment has proved a success, inasmuch as the constitution and stamina of the herd have been established, and all the characteristics of the old animals preserved. The herd now consists of 5 bulls, 4 steers, 9 cows, 8 heifers and 1 heifer calf.'

The type of horn in the Chartley Cattle differs considerably from those of Cadzow and Chillingham, as shown in Plate 41. The ears and muzzle are black.

A few survivors of a polled breed of White Cattle still exist or did till recently, at Blickling Hall, and also at Somerford Park, Cheshire, and some which have been crossed with shorthorns or other breeds, are at Woodbastwick near Norwich, and Vaynol, North Wales.

Many other fine herds of White Wild Cattle at one time flourishing in various parts of England and Scotland, are now extinct.

Pl.40

Wild Cattle. "Cadjow;

Plate 41

Family BOVIDAE Genus BOS

Wild White Cattle
Bos taurus, Linnaeus
pl. 41

It is difficult to trace with any certainty the origin of the so-called 'Wild' Cattle living under semi-feral conditions today, and now considered by most authorities to be descended in all probability from domestic animals which had escaped from captivity at some remote period, and after sheltering for an unknown time in our forests as truly wild creatures, were driven into enclosures in medieval times.

It is therefore a question whether they should be included in a work of this kind, but as the history of the different breeds is of some interest a short account of the principal herds is given.

Mr Millais considers (*Mammals of Great Britain and Ireland*, vol. iii. p. 188) that 'there is a strong probability that the 'Wild' Cattle and all our domestic cattle are descended from breeds produced on the Continent, and that these, after centuries of domestication elsewhere, were introduced into Britain. As far as we can guess, these breeds originally came from the Urus, but at so remote a date that the very earliest history and pictures can give no clue.'

An early domesticated Ox, known as *Bos longifrons*, whose bones have been found in large numbers along with the flint implements of ancient Britons, is said to be the origin of our small Welsh and Highland Cattle.

Though Darwin and other naturalists considered our Park Cattle to be most likely directly descended from the Urus, Professor Owen, Dr J. A. Smith, E. R. Alston and others do not hold this view, but look upon them as originally a domestic breed, whose wildness has been partly due to their environment.

According to Mr Harting (*Extinct British Animals*, p. 220) White Cattle *with red ears* are referred to in the Welsh laws of Howell Dha about A.D. 940 and Wild Cattle are mentioned in the forest laws of King Canute (A.D. 1014–35).

Again they are included among other wild beasts inhabiting the great forests around London by Fitz-Stephen about 1174. In the great Caledonian woods of Central Scotland, pure white forest bulls, with manes like lions, are described by Hector Boece, which may possibly have been the ancestors of the herd which at one time existed at Blair Athole.

As the land became more settled and the forests began to disappear, what were left of the cattle in various parts of Britain were driven into enclosures belonging to the great landed proprietors, where they still remain in one or two localities at the present day.

Perhaps the best known and most famous of the remaining herds is the one at Chillingham Castle, Northumberland, owned by the Earl of Tankerville, where the park extends to about 1100 acres. This enclosure is referred to as far back as 1292 as containing wild animals, apparently those which had been driven in from the surrounding district.

In Plate 41 I have shown the head of a Chillingham Bull drawn from life.

In this breed the horns turn upwards and inwards, the inside of the ears and upper part of the muzzle are reddish brown, and the rest of the animal creamy white.

In Mr Storer's *Wild White Cattle of Great Britain*, pp. 156–157, is given an interesting account of the habits of the Chillingham herd by the late Lord Tankerville, from which the following is quoted: 'They have, in the first place, pre-eminently all the characteristics of wild animals, with some peculiarities that are sometimes very curious and amusing.

'They hide their young and feed in the night, basking or sleeping during the day.

'They are fierce when pressed, but generally speaking very timorous, moving off on the appearance of anyone even at a great distance; yet this varies very much in different seasons of the year, and according to the manner in which they are approached. In summer I have been for several weeks at a time without getting a sight of them – they, on the slightest appearance of anyone, retiring into a wood which serves them as a sanctuary. . . .

'It is observable of them, as of red deer, that they have a peculiar faculty of taking advantage of the irregularities of the ground, so that on being disturbed they may traverse the whole park, and yet you hardly get a sight of them.'

The Chillingham Cattle have not always been distinguished by their reddish-brown ears, as in 1692 the majority are said to have been black-eared, and when Bewick wrote, a few of this type still existed.

Cadzow Castle, Lanarkshire, owned by the Duke of Hamilton, has another fine herd of White Cattle in the park including part of the ancient Caledonian Forest. This forest was formerly used as a hunting ground by the Scottish kings and still retained many of its fine old trees when I saw it some years ago.

In this breed the animals have black ears and muzzle, the legs and feet are spotted with the same colour and the horns are rather more spreading than those of the Chillingham herd.

They show a good many wild traits in their habits and are dangerous if approached too closely.

Their appearance is very striking when seen among their wild surroundings of natural forest.

A bull and cow of the breed are shown on Plate 40.

Chartley Park, Staffordshire, was the home of an ancient herd of White Cattle until 1905. I am indebted to the Duke of Bedford for kindly supplying me with the following particulars of this interesting breed at the present time (January 21, 1921): 'The Chartley Herd (at Woburn). Owner, The Duke of Bedford, K.G., Woburn Abbey, Bedfordshire. This herd is said to have been driven into Chartley Park from the royal forest of Needwood in the reign of Henry III, where they remained until May 1905, when they were bought by the Duke of Bedford. At that time they only numbered seven, and unfortunately they died without leaving any pure bred progeny. Finding that there was no hope of saving the pure bred stock, their new owner crossed a bull with Longhorn cows. This experiment has proved a success, inasmuch as the constitution and stamina of the herd have been established, and all the characteristics of the old animals preserved. The herd now consists of 5 bulls, 4 steers, 9 cows, 8 heifers and 1 heifer calf.'

The type of horn in the Chartley Cattle differs considerably from those of Cadzow and Chillingham, as shown in Plate 41. The ears and muzzle are black.

A few survivors of a polled breed of White Cattle still exist or did till recently, at Blickling Hall, and also at Somerford Park, Cheshire, and some which have been crossed with shorthorns or other breeds, are at Woodbastwick near Norwich, and Vaynol, North Wales.

Many other fine herds of White Wild Cattle at one time flourishing in various parts of England and Scotland, are now extinct.

Pl. 41.

Chillingham Bull.

Chartley Bull.

Wild White Cattle
[Chartley Cattle drawn by Thorburn as a tail-piece to the
description in the 1920–1 edition]

Order CETACEA, whales, dolphins, and porpoises

Though externally the form of the various species of Whales and Dolphins is fashioned in the likeness of a fish, when we come to examine their internal structure and habits, we find this resemblance is only superficial, and that they are really warm-blooded animals, wonderfully adapted to an aquatic existence, bringing forth and suckling their young like other mammals, and requiring to draw their breath from the atmosphere by rising to the surface at frequent intervals.

To facilitate this movement, the tail is made to act as a powerful propeller, and is characterised by having the flukes or blades arranged horizontally and not in an upright position, as in the tail of a fish.

The well-known spout of a whale is merely the exhausted air driven from the lungs, and being warm and moist has the appearance of a fountain of fine spray as it meets the outer and colder atmosphere, when respiration takes place; but should the animal blow just before reaching the surface, water is driven upwards as well. About half an hour is said to be the length of time a whale can remain under water, though they usually come to the surface at much shorter intervals. The longest stay of a Greenland Whale observed by Scoresby was 56 minutes.

The fore limbs or flippers are outwardly formed like paddles, and only capable of movement at the shoulder joint, but hidden within their structure they have an arrangement of bones and muscles not unlike those of the human hand and arm; while the hind legs, represented only by small rudimentary thigh bones, have no outward development, and are buried deep within the body.

The head, especially in the Whalebone Whales, is large in proportion to the body, and joins the latter without any perceptible neck.

The skin is very smooth and glossy, and covers the layer of fat and tissue known as 'blubber', which serves instead of a coat of hair to retain the heat of the body.

The larger species, such as the Blue Whale, measuring up to 85 feet or more in length, with a girth of 40 feet, exceed in their vast size and strength any other animal either of today or prehistoric times.

The food of all the Cetacea, except the Killer (*Orca gladiator*), which often preys on other whales or on seals, consists of fish and small crustaceans, the latter being sometimes of minute size.

The pursuit of the Whale in the Middle Ages supported a brave and hardy race of seamen, and while the old methods of capture have changed, and the hand-thrown harpoon is now superseded by a formidable weapon with an explosive charge attached to it, the industry is still carried on with profit.

Following Sir William Flower, the British Cetacea may be divided into two sub-orders, namely, the Baleen or Whalebone Whales (*Mystacoceti*) and the Toothed Whales (*Odontoceti*). The first of these very distinct types includes the Atlantic Right Whale, the Humpbacked Whale, and the four species of Rorqual; the latter, the Sperm Whale, Bottle-nosed Whale, Cuvier's Whale, Sowerby's Whale, True's Whale, Narwhal, White Whale, Killer, Pilot Whale, Risso's Grampus, Porpoise, and the four Dolphins.

The Greenland or Arctic Right Whale (*Balaena mysticetus*), which appears to be confined entirely to the Polar seas, has never been taken in British waters. This is one of the most valuable of all the species, not only on account of the size and quality of the baleen, but also for the rich supply of oil furnished by the blubber. For this reason it was persistently hunted, after the discovery of its haunts, around the shores of Spitzbergen, first by the English, assisted by Basque harpooners in 1611, and later by other European nations.

Besides being of superior value, the Greenland Whale was easier to capture and kill than its near relation the Atlantic Right Whale of more temperate seas, and this ultimately nearly led to the extinction of the species.

It is worth noting that, although the early whale hunters were well aware of the distinctness of the two species, in later days when the Atlantic Right Whale had almost disappeared in European waters, they were confused and classed as the same animal.

Even William Scoresby, a whaler of great experience, as well as a man of high scientific attainments, who penetrated farther north than any of his predecessors, never met with the more southern species, and did not believe in its existence. His book on the Arctic Regions, published in 1820, gives the best known account of the Greenland Whale fishing, and is full of interesting facts.

The Danish cetologists Eschricht and Reinhardt were the first in modern times to point out the difference between the Greenland and Atlantic Right Whales. The Right Whales were so named because they were the most profitable kind to hunt on account of their valuable baleen and large yield of oil, and they were also less difficult to kill than the Rorquals and others.

Plate 42

Sub-Order MYSTACOCETI, the whalebone whales
Family BALAENIDAE Genus BALAENA

The Atlantic Right Whale
Balaena australis, Desmoulins
pl. 42 **top**

The Atlantic Right Whale or Nordcaper, known to the French as Sarde, measures over 50 feet when fully grown.

According to Professor D'Arcy Wentworth Thompson, C.B., F.R.S. (*Scottish Naturalist*, Sept. 1918), of sixty-seven specimens captured and brought into the Scottish Whaling Stations during the years from 1908 to 1914, the smallest measured 31 feet and the largest 59 feet, but it is not certain whether these measurements were taken along the curve of the animal's bodies or in a straight line. The average girth of twenty-two specimens was about 32 feet.

Outwardly this Whale chiefly differs from the Greenland Right Whale in having a smaller head, shorter and thicker baleen, while the curved margin of the lower lip follows a different line.

Along the top of the upper jaw, which slopes steeply from where the blow holes are placed in the crown, is a rough horny mass known as the 'bonnet'.

The head is large, measuring about one-fourth of the animal's entire length, the body short and thick-set with no dorsal fin, and tapering rapidly towards the tail.

The colour is entirely black.

During the Middle Ages this was a common species in the Bay of Biscay and English Channel, and westwards was plentiful in the Atlantic round the coasts of Newfoundland. Later on, it became increasingly scarce in its old haunts, and towards the middle of last century and for some time later, appeared to be almost extinct. However, between 1889 and 1891 about seventeen were taken by the Norwegian whalers off Iceland, and as already mentioned sixty-seven were captured and brought to the Scottish stations between 1908 and 1914.

Professor D'Arcy Wentworth Thompson has shown in his interesting account of the whales landed at these ports (*Scottish Naturalist*, Sept. 1918, pp. 204–205), that nearly all the Nord-capers were brought into Buneaveneader, having been 'caught within a limited area lying to the west and south-west of the Hebrides and beyond St Kilda, as far as about 10° W. None have been taken on the Rockall grounds and very few in the neighbourhood of the Shetlands.' Right Whales, separated from the Atlantic Right Whale by differences so slight as to make them appear identical, inhabit the South Atlantic as well as the North and South Pacific.

The pursuit of the Nordcaper can be traced far back in the Middle Ages, and appears to have been first carried on by the Basques in the Bay of Biscay, along the coasts of France and Spain, when the whale hunters were able to bring in their captures to Bayonne, Biarritz, San Sebastian and other ports.

In course of time, the whales becoming scarce near shore, they were followed across the Atlantic as far as the coast of Newfoundland, where an extensive fishery was carried on.

These Biscayan Whalers were fine intrepid seamen, skilful in the use of the weapon they invented, which still bears the name they gave it of 'harpoon', and when the first English seamen under Thomas Edge went north to Spitzbergen in 1611 to hunt the Greenland Whale, they found it necessary to take six Basque harpooners among the crew.

When feeding, the Nordcaper opens its capacious mouth as it proceeds slowly under the surface of the sea, then closing the jaws when the inrush of water has drawn in a multitude of minute crustaceans, it expels the liquid through the baleen blades, while the food remains on the tongue. The amount of nourishment thus taken in must be vast, to supply the needs of such an animal.

The old-fashioned method of hunting the whale with hand-thrown harpoons from boats in touch with a vessel, has now been superseded by an entirely new system, first practised by the Norwegians, when Svend Foyn invented a new weapon in 1864 in order to cope with the dangerous Rorquals. This was a heavy harpoon, with an explosive charge, attached to a strong rope and fired from a gun mounted in the bow of a steamship of moderate size. This method was found to be very efficient.

According to Scoresby a harpoon-gun was in use as far back as 1731, but this was discharged from a small boat at close quarters and was not altogether a success.

In modern whaling, if the animal is not killed by the shock caused by the harpoon, it is soon brought to the surface and killed by being lanced from a boat.

According to Millais (*Mammals of Great Britain and Ireland*), 'Right Whales bring forth in the month of March every other year, the young being suckled for twelve months.'

For the drawing of this species in the Plate, and for some of the others, I have used the models in the British Museum (Natural History).

Family BALAENOPTERIDAE Genus MEGAPTERA

The Humpbacked Whale
Megaptera boöps, Fabricius
pl. 42 **bottom**

The Humpbacked Whale, the only representative of its genus, is characterised by its stout massive body, low dorsal fin, and extraordinary length of the usually glistering white flippers. In form the latter are narrow, slightly curved, and deeply indented along the outer and part of their inner margins. The throat and chest are grooved with long furrows to allow the necessary expansion of these parts, when the mouth is filled with water containing the small fishes and crustaceans on which the animal lives.

In this species these furrows are set farther apart and are less numerous than in the Rorquals. The baleen is short and black in colour.

About the region of the snout and lower lips are some small knobs or tubercles. In the skeleton the seven vertebrae of the neck are free, and not fused together as in the Right Whales.

The upper parts of the Humpbacked Whale are black in colour, but the under surface varies considerably in different specimens, sometimes this is white, sometimes black, or often a combination of both colours.

There is also a good deal of variation in the colour of the outer side of the flippers, which may be pure white, white varied with irregular black markings, or black with white patches, but they are always white underneath. In length this species measures from 45 to 50 feet, while the girth is very great in comparison with the length.

The males are usually less than the females.

The Humpback has an extremely wide distribution and visits more or less every part of the Atlantic and Pacific Oceans.

In British waters the majority of the captures of this whale have occurred of late years north of the Shetlands and about St Kilda.

In character the Humpback is usually bold and fearless and will often allow a close approach by boats and vessels. Mr Millais describes it as 'a gay and sportive animal, frequently springing out of the water and engaging in uncouth gambols'.

Sometimes it may be seen lying on its side or rolling over on its back on the surface of the water.

Owing to its great activity and fighting propensities the Humpback is considered a dangerous animal to tackle, and it was generally left alone by whalers until the modern method of attack was invented. Even now the successful lancing of this species from a small boat is usually a difficult and dangerous operation.

The females show great affection for their young and will defend them with their lives. The food consists of small fishes, squids, and crustaceans.

Pl. 42.

Atlantic Right Whale.

Humbacked Whale.

Plate 43

Genus BALAENOPTERA

Sibbald's Rorqual or Blue Whale
Balaenoptera sibbaldii, Gray
pl. 43 **bottom**

The Rorquals, also called Fin Whales, Finbacks or Finners, by whalers, are characterised by their extenuated bodies, rather small and pointed heads, comparatively small flippers, and the large number of longitudinal furrows on the throat and under parts. The dorsal fin is falcated.

The seven vertebrae of the neck are free.

The Blue Whale, as the largest of this group is now usually named, exceeds in size any known animal and measures up to 85 feet and occasionally more in total length.

Millais mentions a monster measuring 102 feet killed by Captain Foden near Derafjord, Iceland, in 1896, and gives the dead weight of the species 'at from one hundred and fifty to two hundred tons'. The same author gives the colour of an adult bull whose chase and capture he witnessed in August 1905 as follows (*Mammals of Great Britain and Ireland*, vol. ii. p. 250): 'The whole of the upper parts were a pale blue-grey, with numerous small brown-grey spots and a few white spots on the neck, shoulders, and flank; tail blue-grey with a white anterior margin; under parts dull brownish grey, being especially dark in the throat and ventral grooves. Pectorals pale bluish grey with the anterior edge white; inner surface and lower convex border pure white; iris pale brown. . . . Tail much spotted with white both above and below.'

This example measured 78 feet.

The baleen plates are black.

Formerly considered uncommon, the Blue Whale is now known to be plentiful in the North Atlantic during favourable seasons, and large numbers have been captured since the modern system of whaling began.

According to Professor D'Arcy Wentworth Thompson, C.B., F.R.S. (*Scottish Naturalist*, October 1918, pp. 230–231), about seven hundred and thirty of this species were captured around Iceland between 1890 and 1901 by Captain L. Berg. From 1908 to 1914 one hundred and nine were brought into the Scottish stations. Of the latter, the smallest measured 42 feet, the largest 85 feet, and most of them were caught to the westwards of St Kilda.

Like the Humpbacked Whale, this species has a very wide range, extending from the Arctic regions throughout the Atlantic and Pacific to the Antarctic seas.

In the summer months large migratory herds appear in the seas about the North Cape and Iceland.

The food of the Blue Whale consists of 'plankton' or 'kril' (masses of small floating crustaceans, etc.) left stranded in the mouth of the animal, after the expulsion of the mouthful of water through the plates of baleen or whalebone.

Owing to its great strength and endurance, this whale was wisely left alone by the early whalers, but since the introduction of the modern harpoon gun, it has been much hunted along with the other Rorquals by the Norwegians.

The marvellous strength and staying power of the Blue Whale can best be realized by those on board ship when the animal takes the vessel in tow, after having been struck by a harpoon and not crippled by the shock of the explosive charge. On occasions, it has been known to drag a steamship through the water for many hours, with the engines at half-speed astern.

The 'spout' of the animal is described by Mr Millais as 'much loftier than that of any other cetacean', and can be seen on a clear day at a distance of several miles. Three which he saw in August 1905, off Newfoundland, frequently spouted to a height of thirty feet.

Unlike the Right Whales and Sperm, the body of the Blue Whale and other Rorquals sinks after death and requires to be hauled to the surface by the strong hawser attached to the harpoon, worked by a winch on board ship.

To keep the carcase afloat, steam is driven into it through a pipe, and when possible it is taken to a station or factory to be cut up.

The whalebone of the Rorquals is of little value compared to that of the Right Whales, but the oil brings a good price, and various products are now obtained from the bones and flesh, the latter being dried, and ground into meal to feed cattle. Combined with the bones, it is also used as a fertiliser.

Like the others of this family, the female Blue Whale carefully tends her calf, until it is able to fend for itself.

The Common Rorqual
Balaenoptera musculus, Linnaeus
pl. 43 **top**

The Common Rorqual, generally called the 'Finner' by whalers, measures when full grown up to 70 and even 80 feet.

The body is remarkably long and slender, with little diminution in the girth of the posterior portion as it approaches the tail, the flippers are small, the dorsal fin prominent and rather triangular in shape.

According to Millais the colour of the upper part 'is not black as usually described, but is always sepia, passing into brownish grey on the flanks. There is great individual variation in this species.'

The underparts are chiefly white, the division between the light and dark colour on the belly being sharply defined. The underside of the flippers is always white.

The baleen plates are variegated with slaty grey and cream colour.

The Common Rorqual inhabits the Atlantic and Pacific Oceans, having much the same distribution as the Blue Whale. It is migratory like the others, and in summer frequents the seas of Scandinavia as well as the neighbourhood of Iceland, and of Greenland.

It is by far the most common of the big whales met within British waters, and appears in large numbers north of the Shetlands, where the chief captures are made. A good many are also taken about St Kilda.

In the Pacific, it is not uncommon at times off the coast of California, while southwards near the Antarctic circle, numbers are caught by the Norwegian whalers about South Georgia and South Shetland.

On account of its speed and fighting spirit, this species is looked upon by whalers as one of the most dangerous kinds to encounter, especially when it is necessary to lance one from a small boat. Whaling vessels have been sunk by Finbacks charging and knocking a hole in their sides, so it is not surprising that the early whale hunters gave them a wide berth.

Describing the danger in attacking the large Rorquals, Scoresby says (*Arctic Regions*, vol. i. pp. 480–481): 'I have made different attempts to capture one of these formidable creatures. In the year 1818, I ordered a chase of them, providing against the danger of having my crew separated from the ship, by appointing a rendezvous on the shore not far distant, and preparing against the loss of much line, by dividing it at 200 fathoms from the harpoon, and affixing a buoy to the end of it. Thus arranged, one of these whales was shot and another struck. The former dived with such impetuosity that the line was broken by the resistance of the buoy as soon as it was thrown into the water, and the latter was liberated within a minute by the division of the line, occasioned, it was supposed, by its friction against the dorsal fin.

'Both of them escaped. Another physalis (Rorqual) was struck by one of my inexperienced harpooners, who mistook it for a mysticetus. It dived obliquely with such velocity that 480 fathoms of line were withdrawn from the boat in about a minute of time. This whale was also lost by the breaking of the line.'

The Common Rorqual feeds on herrings and other fish as well as on crustaceans and squids.

Pl. 43.

Common Rorqual

Sibbald's Rorqual or Blue Whale. 80.

Plate 44   Genus HYPEROÖDON

Rudolphi's Rorqual
Balaenoptera borealis, Lesson
pl. 44 **bottom**

The Sei-Whale (Saithe-Whale), as this species is called by whalers, was first described by the Italian naturalist Rudolphi from a specimen taken in the Baltic in 1819. It is smaller than the Common Rorqual, full grown specimens measuring between 50 and 60 feet in length and occasionally more.

The flippers are relatively short, the dorsal fin high and falcate and placed well forward on the body.

Rudolphi's Rorqual varies considerably in colour.

Mr Millais says (*Mammals of Great Britain and Ireland*), 'The majority are dark sepia suffused with grey like *B. musculus*. The colour of the under surface is grey with large irregular patches of white, the parts about the throat and genital organs white, from thence backwards to the flukes grey.'

Collett gives the colour of the upper parts as 'dark blue grey'. It should be borne in mind that the effect of outdoor light gives the smooth shining backs of all these whales a bluish cast. The baleen blades, which are of considerable value as whalebone, are black in colour, with the bristly parts yellowish white.

Little was known about this Rorqual till the Norwegians started their whaling stations about the North Cape in the early 'eighties' of last century, when it was found to be a regular visitor to these northern waters in the summer months.

In 1885 no less than 771 were taken off the coast of Finmark, and large catches have been obtained in recent years in the neighbourhood of St Kilda and north of the Shetlands. From May till August it appears to be common in some seasons in these northern waters, but according to Flower and Lydekker it has not been found south of Biarritz.

Westwards it is plentiful at times on the coasts of Newfoundland and Labrador.

In habits this species does not appear to differ much from the other Rorquals, but it may be distinguished when at the surface of the water by the fairly large falcate dorsal fin.

According to Collett, its food consists of small crustaceans.

The Lesser Rorqual
Balaenoptera acuto-rostrata, Lacépède
pl. 44 **top**

The Lesser Rorqual, also known as the Pike-whale, is distinguished from the rest of the *Balaenoptera* by its much smaller size and also by the white band across the upper side of the flippers. It measures up to about 30 feet in length, is somewhat stout in build and like Rudolphi's Rorqual possesses a rather high and hooked dorsal fin.

The colour above is greyish black or brownish grey, the ribbed underparts are white and the baleen yellowish white.

This whale is a northern species, approaching in summer the ice floes of the Polar regions, when it also visits the fjords of Norway, the Shetlands, and the coasts of Scotland.

It has more often been stranded on the shores of Scotland than those of England.

In the *Report on Cetacea Stranded on the British Coasts during 1916*, by Sir Sidney Harmer, F.R.S., two Lesser Rorquals are reported stranded on the Scottish Coasts, one at North Berwick in August and another at Caithness in October. The first of these had lost its head, tail, and flippers.

The habits of this species are not known to differ from those of its congeners, and owing to its small size it is not considered of much value by the whalers.

The Bottle-nosed Whale
Hyperoödon rostratum, Müller
pls. 44 **right** and 45 **top**

This species possesses a single pair of teeth, which are hidden in the gum at the point of the lower mandible, and are invisible in the living animal.

The snout is lengthened in the form of a pronounced beak; above this the frontal part of the head rises, in the old males almost perpendicularly, but in the females and young with a more sloping outline. The adult males attain a length of 30 feet, the females about 24 feet.

The bones of the neck are united. The flippers and dorsal fin are small, the latter being placed far back.

The drawing of the head of this Whale (Plate 44) taken from a cast in the British Museum (Natural History) shows one of the gular grooves, a pair of which run along the lower jaw.

The Bottle-nosed Whale shows great variation in its colour.

According to Captain D. Gray (*Proceedings of the Zoological Society for 1882*), 'They vary in colour from black in the young to light brown in the older animals. The very old turn almost yellow, the beak and front part of the head being nearly white, with a white band round their necks; all of them are greyish white on the belly.'

The species is found in considerable numbers in the North Atlantic, and it penetrates as far as the margin of the ice in the Arctic seas. It is abundant in the waters on both the western and eastern sides of Greenland, from thence across to Spitzbergen, Iceland, and the British Islands, where it has often been found cast on our coasts.

The food is said to consist chiefly of cuttlefish. Captain D. Gray, in his account of this species referred to above, describes its food as 'a bluish white cuttlefish, six inches long by three inches in circumference, and pointed towards the tail'.

On account of the value of its oil and spermaceti, the Bottle-nose has been much hunted, though it appears to be one of the most dangerous of whales to harpoon from a boat, because of the sudden downward rush which the animal makes when struck, and unless great attention is given to the line, men are liable to get entangled and swept overboard. Many accidents have happened in this way. There is also the danger of the whole boat and its crew being dragged under should any hitch occur and the line not instantly cut.

The Bottle-nose is sociable in its habits, moving about in small parties or 'schools'.

According to Captain D. Gray's above mentioned account, 'They are very unsuspicious, coming close alongside the ship, round about underneath the boats, until their curiosity is satisfied. . . . They can leap many feet out of the water, even having time while in the air to turn round their heads and look about them, taking the water head first, and not falling into it sideways like the larger whales.'

Pl. 44.

Bottle-nosed Whale. $\frac{1}{11}$.

Rudolphi's Rorqual. $\frac{1}{60}$.

Lesser Rorqual

Plate 45

Family PHYSETERIDAE Genus PHYSETER
Sub-Order ODONTOCETI, toothed whales

The Sperm Whale or Cachalot
Physeter macrocephalus, Linnaeus
pl. 45 **bottom**

The various members of this group (*Odontoceti*) are distinguished by the possession of teeth, which may be numerous in both upper and lower jaws, or confined to a single pair in the latter; there is also no whalebone. The nostrils are united below the surface and form one external blowhole. The skull is not symmetrical.

The Sperm, by far the largest of these toothed whales, measures up to and over 60 feet, the females being considerably less. The huge head, appearing as if cut off abruptly in front, and taking up about one-third of the whole length of the body, is curiously shaped, the massive upper part being adapted as a sort of well or receptacle to contain the valuable oily fluid known as spermaceti. The blowhole is placed very far forward on the left-hand side and near the extremity of the head. The first vertebra of the neck is free, the others united.

The upper jaw reaches considerably beyond the lower.

One or more rounded protuberances on the back represent the dorsal fin.

The flippers are broad and unpointed. In the lower jaw are from twenty to twenty-five pairs of hooked teeth, those in the upper jaw being rudimentary and buried in the gum.

In colour, the upper parts of this whale are black or greyish black, the underparts much lighter and greyer.

The blubber of the Cachalot, as the Sperm Whale is frequently called, furnishes the valuable sperm oil of commerce, and the great reservoir in the head or 'case', contains the spermaceti. The latter is a clear oily liquid which can be bailed out while warm, but afterwards hardens to a white waxy substance.

Another valuable product of this animal is Ambergris, a secretion found in its stomach or sometimes floating in the water. Mr W. G. Burn Murdoch (*Modern Whaling and Bear Hunting*, p. 314) describes it as 'a solid fatty substance of a marbled grey-and-black appearance, and generally contains the beaks of cuttle-fish, which form the principal food of the Cachalot or Sperm Whale. When fresh it has an intolerable smell, but after exposure this goes and leaves what some people call a "peculiar sweet earthy odour".'

Ambergris is used as a basis in the manufacture of perfumes and brings a great price, as much as twenty-five shillings an ounce.

The Sperm Whale has a wide distribution throughout the warmer waters of the world, inhabiting the Pacific, Indian, and Atlantic oceans and travelling in large bands or 'schools'.

From time to time it gets stranded on the coasts of the British Islands.

One of the earliest recorded is that by Sir Thomas Browne, who mentions a 'spermaceti whale' stranded at Hunstanton, Norfolk, early in the seventeenth century. An earlier record, which seems to refer to this species, may be found in Sir R. Baker's *Chronicle*, published in 1650. In this the statement is made that 'In her seventeenth year (*Queen Elizabeth's*, 1575) a vast mighty whale was cast upon the Isle of Thanet in Kent twenty ells long, and thirteen foot broad from the belly to the back-bone, and eleven foot between the eyes. . . . The oil being boyled out of his head was *Parmacittee*.'

The first recorded Scottish example was taken at Limekilns, Firth of Forth, in 1689.

Most of the captures of Sperm Whales on our side of the Atlantic have occurred in recent years about St Kilda and Rockall, where, according to Professor D'Arcy Wentworth Thompson (*Scottish Naturalist*, Oct. 1918, p. 222), forty-two were taken during the years 1908–1914, all being males except one.

Thomas Beale, in his work on the Natural History of the Sperm Whale, as quoted by Millais, describes it as 'moving through the water with the greatest ease, and with considerable velocity. When undisturbed, he passes tranquilly along just below the surface of the water at the rate of about three or four miles an hour, which motion he effects by a gentle oblique motion from side to side of the flukes, precisely in the same manner as a boat is sculled by means of an oar over the stern. When proceeding at this, his common rate, his body lies horizontally, his hump projecting above the surface, with the water a little disturbed around it, and more or less so according to his velocity; this disturbed water is called by whalers 'white water', and from the greater or less quantity of it an experienced whaler can judge very accurately of the rate at which a whale is going from a distance of even four or five miles.

'In this mode of swimming the whale is able to attain a velocity of about seven miles an hour, but when desirous of proceeding at a greater rate the action of the tail is materially altered; instead of being moved laterally and obliquely, it strikes the water with the broad flat surface of the flukes in a direct manner, upwards and downwards; and each time the blow is made with the inferior surface, the head of the whale sinks down to the depth of eight or ten feet, but when the blow is reversed it rises out of the water, presenting then to it only the sharp cutwater-like inferior portion.'

Describing the spout of this species, Millais says: 'After an absence under water of from twenty minutes to one hour, the Sperm Whale rises to blow. The form of the spout is different, both in the form and in the angle at which it is projected, from that of any other Cetacean. The column of vapour lasts about three seconds, and is shot out from the blowhole at an angle of 35° for a distance of 15 to 20 feet, the spray falling like a fountain, but if any wind is blowing it appears "bushy".' Owing to the forward position of the nostril the spout is projected from the extremity of the snout.

The Sperm Whale is polygamous, and while the strongest bulls take possession of the cows, the younger males are driven out and roam the seas in herds.

According to the late Frank Bullen, the female Cachalot shows less consideration for her young than the other large Whales, and will desert it when attacked.

Before the introduction of the modern method of capture, the Sperm was considered a dangerous whale to harpoon, as when defending itself it used its powerful jaws as well as the great tail flukes, which often caused fatal accidents in this pursuit. The food consists chiefly of squids, including some of great size, and also of various fishes.

Genus HYPEROÖDON

The Bottle-nosed Whale
Hyperoödon rostratum, Müller
pl. 45 **top**
see description on page 100

Pl.45.

Bottle-nosed Whale.

Sperm Whale.

Plate 46

Genus ZIPHIUS

Cuvier's Whale
Ziphius cavirostris
pl. 46 **bottom**

This rare beaked Whale, the only known species of the genus *Ziphius*, is distinguished by the single pair of pointed teeth inclining forwards at the extreme end of the lower jaw. In the skeleton, only the first three vertebrae of the neck are joined, the others being free. Until recently very little was known of the appearance and colour of Cuvier's Whale. It was first described by the scientist whose name it bears from a skull obtained on the coast of Southern France, and a few more examples have been obtained at long intervals in the Mediterranean and one in Sweden.

The first British specimen was captured off Hamna Voe, Shetland, in 1870, whose skull on being sent to Edinburgh was identified by Sir William Turner.

On July 18th, 1915, a good example of a male Cuvier's Whale came ashore at Fethard, Co. Wexford, Ireland, and, thanks to a recent Government regulation whereby any whale stranded on our coasts is immediately reported by the coast-guard to the authorities at the British Museum of Natural History, an exact model of the specimen was able to be made on the spot, and the colours and measurements noted by Mr Bishop.

This whale measured 18 feet 2½ inches in total length. In colour the area from the chin to the base of dorsal fin was greenish white, the rest of the body slaty black. As usual in whales whose food consists chiefly of squids, the flanks of the animal were marked with various lines and scratches caused by the tentacles of these creatures. In life the colour of the light parts of the head and shoulders was probably a purer white, as Mr W. P. Pycraft, to whom I am indebted for many useful notes on the cetaceans, tells me that he once observed two Cuvier's Whales in the sea off the Wexford coast, and while watching them from above was struck with the shining white-ness of the head and shoulders as the animals moved through the clear water. According to Sir Sidney Harmer's *Report on Cetacea Stranded on the British Coasts during 1916*, an example of this species occurred on the Cornish coast on June 7th of that year.

Cuvier's Whale has an extremely wide distribution, roving from the British coasts and those of the Mediterranean through the Atlantic, India, and Pacific Oceans to New Zealand, where it has been obtained on several occasions. A young New Zealand *Ziphius*, described by Messrs Scott and Parker in the *Transactions of the Zoological Society*, vol. xii, was coloured brown on the sides of the head and purple black on the back. The drawing in the Plate was made from the model in the British Museum (Natural History).

Sowerby's Whale
Mesoplodon bidens, Sowerby
pl. 46 **top**

In this genus, comprising several species – only two of which are British – the snout is elongated in the form of a beak, and in Sowerby's Whale the adult male is characterised by a single pair of pointed teeth placed rather far back in the lower man-dible towards the middle of the jaw, while in True's Beaked Whale they are situated at the extremity of the lower mandible. Sowerby's Whale measures from 15 to 18 feet in length, and in colour is usually a bluish black all over the body, with many criss-cross lines and scratches on its surface, caused by the tentacles of cuttlefish.

The following is the description of the colour in a female specimen stranded on the Norfolk coast at Overstrand, near Cromer, in December 1892, by the late Thomas Southwell and Dr Harmer – now Sir Sidney Harmer – in the *Annals and Magazine of Natural History* (ser. 6, vol. xi, April 1893): 'Previous observers have described this animal as being lighter beneath than above. This was distinctly not the case in the specimen under consideration, which was of a uniform black colour (with the slight exception shortly to be mentioned), the skin being very smooth and polished, as has been described in other instances; and the fishermen in charge who had assisted in its capture informed us that there was a perceptible bluish tint on the skin in a good light.

'But the most remarkable feature was the presence of a number of curiously shaped marks sparsely distributed over the body, but most conspicuous on the side and ventral surface. These spots were most irregular in size and figure, others mere blotches, others again having the appearance of splashes or smears varying in size up to that of a man's hand.'

The first example of Sowerby's Whale known to naturalists, which was described by Sowerby, was obtained on the shores of the Moray Firth near Nairn in 1800.

Since that date others have come ashore from time to time, mostly in Scotland, and the latest I know of is one obtained on the Lincolnshire coast mentioned in Sir Sidney Harmer's *Report on Cetacea Stranded on the British Coasts during 1916*.

The knowledge of the distribution of Sowerby's Whale is meagre. It has been taken on the coasts of Scandinavia, whence it ranges as far as Australia and New Zealand in the Pacific.

True's Beaked Whale
Mesoplodon mirus
(not shown)

An example of this very rare beaked whale – first described by the late W. F. True in 1913 (True, 1913, *Proc. U.S. Nat. Mus.*, xlv. pl. 51), from a specimen taken at Beaufort Harbour, North Carolina – was obtained at Liscannor, County Clare, Ireland, on June 9th, 1917. Another is said to have been stranded in Galway Bay about 1899.

This species appears to be closely related to Sowerby's Whale, but the characteristic pair of teeth in True's Beaked Whale are placed at the point of the lower jaw as in Cuvier's Whale.

I am indebted to Mr W. P. Pycraft for the above mentioned particulars.

Pl. 46.

Sowerby's Whale.
Cuvier's Whale.

$\frac{1}{25}$.

Plate 47

Family DELPHINIDAE Genus MONODON

The Narwhal
Monodon monoceros, Linnaeus
pl. 47 **bottom**

The members of this family (*Delphinidae*) are characterised by usually possessing a number of teeth in both jaws.

As a rule the different species are much smaller than in the Physeteridae, though the Killer attains a length of about 30 feet. The blowhole takes the form of a crescent, with the points directed forwards.

The Narwhal or 'Unicorn' of the whalers, attains a length of from 13 to 16 feet, excluding the tusk, and its widest circumference is 8 to 9 feet, according to Scoresby. The tusk or 'horn', peculiar to the male, tapers to a blunt point and has a spiral twist from left to right. It measures from 5 to 8 feet in length, and has its origin on the lower part of the left hand side of the upper jaw. The right hand tusk is usually rudimentary and concealed in the jaw.

In the female the tusk is undeveloped, but both sexes have also some rudimentary teeth.

On rare occasions a pair of tusks are developed in the male.

Scoresby gives the following description of the species (*Arctic Regions*, vol. i. pp. 487–494): 'The head is about one-seventh of the whole length of the animal; it is small, blunt, round, and of a paraboloidal form. The mouth is small and not capable of much extension. The under lip is wedge-shaped. The eyes are small, the largest diameter being only an inch, and are placed in a line with the opening of the mouth, about 13 inches from the snout. The blowhole, which is directly over the eyes, is a single opening, of a semi-circular form, about $3\frac{1}{2}$ inches in diameter or breadth, and $1\frac{1}{2}$ radius or length.

'The fins, which are 12 or 14 inches long and 6 or 8 broad, are placed one-fifth of the length of the animal from the snout. The tail is from 15 to 20 inches long, and 3 to 4 feet broad. It has no dorsal fin, but in place of it is an irregular sharpish fatty ridge, 2 inches in height, extending $2\frac{1}{2}$ feet along the back, nearly midway between the snout and the tail. The edge of this ridge is generally rough, and the cuticle and rete mucosum being partly wanting upon it, appear to be worn off by rubbing against the ice.

'The prevailing colour of the young Narwhal is blackish-grey on the back, variegated with numerous darker spots running into one another, and forming a dusky black surface, paler and more open spots of grey on a white ground at the sides, disappearing altogether about the middle of the belly. In the elder animals the ground is wholly white or yellowish-white, with dark-grey or blackish spots of different degrees of intensity. These spots are of a roundish or oblong form: on the back, where they seldom exceed two inches in diameter, they are the darkest and most crowded together, yet with intervals of pure white among them. On the sides, the spots are fainter, smaller, and more open. On the belly, they become extremely faint and few, and in considerable surfaces are not to be seen.

'On the upper part of the neck, just behind the blowhole, is often a close patch of brownish-black without any white.

'The external part of the fins is also generally black at the edges, but greyish about the middle. The upper side of the tail is also blackish round the edges, but in the middle, grey, with black curvilinear streaks on a white ground, forming semi-circular figures on each lobe. . . . The colour of the sucklings is almost wholly a bluish-grey or slate-colour. . . .

'The principal food of the Narwhal seems to be molluscous animals. In the stomachs of several that I have examined were numerous remains of sepiae.

'Narwhals are quick, active, inoffensive animals. They swim with considerable velocity. When respiring at the surface, they frequently lie motionless for several minutes, with their backs and heads just appearing above water. They are of a somewhat gregarious disposition, often appearing in numerous little herds of half a dozen, or more, together. Each herd is most frequently composed of animals of the same sex.'

According to Mr W. G. Burn Murdoch (*Modern Whaling and Bear Hunting*, p. 237) Narwhals utter at times a groaning sound.

This species keeps chiefly to the ice in the Arctic seas, and only on very rare occasions has visited the British coasts.

The first is recorded from the Firth of Forth, where one was taken near the Isle of May as far back as 1648. The next was stranded alive near Boston, Lincolnshire, in 1800, and another was driven ashore in Weisdale Sound, Shetland, in September 1808.

Genus DELPHINAPTERUS

The White Whale or Beluga
Delphinapterus leucas, Pallas
pl. 47 **top**

This other Arctic species, nearly related to the Narwhal, measures from 12 to 20 feet in length. The forehead is full and rounded. The jaws contain from eight to ten teeth on each side. There is no back fin, but its place is occupied by a low ridge. The skin is smooth, in colour a glossy yellowish white in the adult, in the young a dark mottled grey.

The White Whale inhabits the waters of the circumpolar region, ranging as far north as 81° 35′, according to Greely. It is abundant north of Iceland and about Spitzbergen, and also frequents the mouths of the great rivers of Northern Siberia. From the Seas around Greenland it ranges on the American side to Labrador, the river St Lawrence and Alaska. This Whale only occasionally visits the British Islands. Two immature examples are said to have been stranded in the Pentland Firth, west of Thurso, in 1793. Another which had previously been noticed for three months in the Firth of Forth, was killed by some fishermen in June 1815. The occurrence of one was recorded in the Island of Auskerry, Orkneys, in October 1845 (Bell).

Alston mentions one seen in Loch Etive in June 1878, and according to Millais another was caught by the flukes of the tail between the two posts of a stake net near the little Ferry, Sutherland, in 1879.

Harvie-Brown and Buckley mention one seen in the Kyle of Tongue in August 1880, and another was taken at Dunbeath, Caithness, in 1884 (Millais).

The White Whale has seldom occurred in England. Millais mentions the capture of two, the first at the mouth of the Tyne, June 1903, and one shot at Moreby on the Yorkshire Ouse.

This species is gregarious and is very lively and playful in its actions, often coming to the surface of the water where it will roll and gambol in the neighbourhood of vessels. Captain Scammon says (*Marine Mammalia and American Whale Fishery*, p. 93): 'When undulating along in this manner, it often makes a noise at the moment of coming to the surface to respire which may be likened to the faint lowing of an ox, but the strain is not so prolonged.'

The White Whale has several times been kept in confinement. Bell mentions one which lived for two years in a tank in America, and two were exhibited at different times at the Westminster Aquarium; these however only lived for a short time.

The skin is of considerable value, being manufactured into the 'porpoise leather' used for boots.

For this reason large numbers are annually killed by the Norwegian Whalers.

The Esquimaux also hunt them for their blubber and flesh.

Pl. 47.

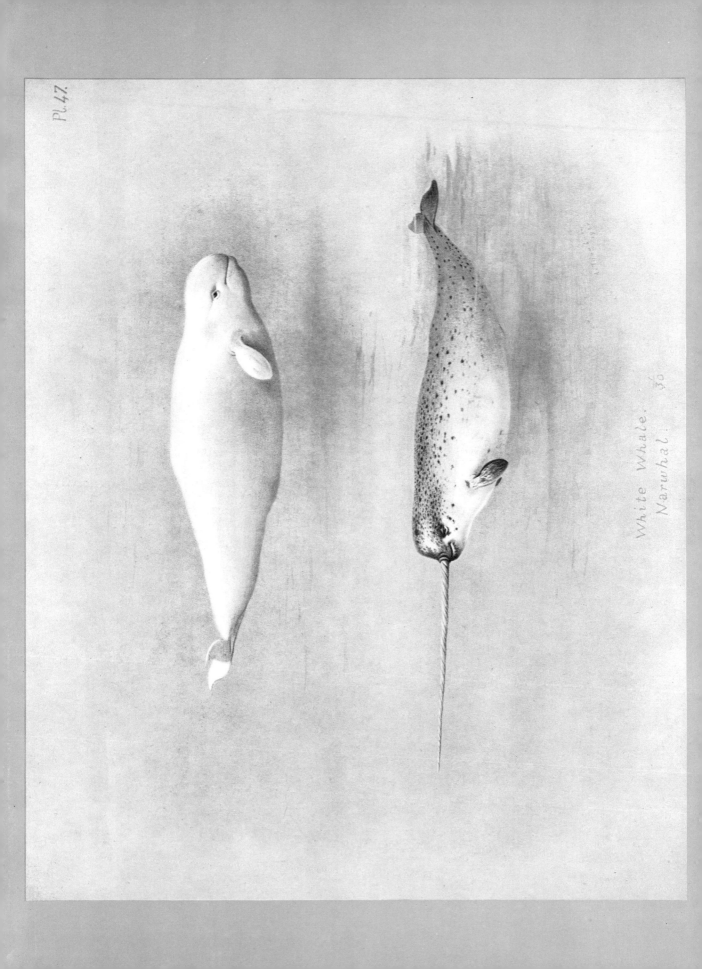

White Whale.
Narwhal. 30

Plate 48

Genus ORCA

The Killer or Grampus
Orca gladiator, Gray
pl. 48 **top**

In this large species, the adult male attains a length of about 30 feet, the female being considerably less. The head is broad and rounded, the jaws contain about twelve pairs of formidable curved teeth, and the whole body is very robust. The most striking feature in this whale is the enormous development of the flippers and dorsal fin in some of the old males. In Sir Sidney Harmer's *Report on Cetaceans Stranded on the British Coasts during 1916*, mention is made of one found in the Solway Firth whose dorsal fin measured no less than 5 feet 6 inches in length, the pectoral fins 6 feet 8 inches in length and 3 feet 7 inches in breadth, the flippers being larger than those in an adult male Sperm Whale.

The flukes of the tail are also very broad and strong.

The upper parts are glossy black in colour, with an elongated white patch extending backwards from just above the eye. The chin, throat, and belly are pure white; this colour is carried upwards in the form of a well defined lobe which overlaps the black on the sides of the animal. Behind the great dorsal fin, which stands erect in the middle of the back, is a grey or purplish saddle mark extending across the body in the form of a crescent. The Killer ranges far through the Atlantic and Pacific Oceans, from the Arctic ice floes to those of the Antarctic.

It often visits the British coasts in summer, especially the more northern parts about the Orkneys and Shetlands, and less frequently the English and Irish shores.

It has been known on several occasions to ascend rivers in England for some considerable distance, even as far up as Chelsea on the Thames, where three were seen in 1890. In character the Killer is fierce and rapacious, and has been likened to the wolf of the seas. They usually roam through the ocean in packs, travelling with great speed, and do not hesitate to attack large animals such as the Greenland Whale and Finner. Mr E. W. Nelson, writing in the *National Geographical Magazine*, Washington, Nov. 1916, p. 468, says: 'Unlike most whales, the members of these schools do not travel in a straggling party, but swim side by side, their movements as regularly timed as those of soldiers. A regularly spaced row of advancing long black fins swiftly cutting the undulating surface of the sea produces a singularly sinister effect.

'The evil impression is well justified, since Killers are the most savage and remorseless of whales.'

In attacking their quarry, if it be one of the larger Whales, the Killers approach it on both sides, and generally endeavour to tear out the tongue when the animal opens its mouth through exhaustion.

Not only are whales and their young preyed upon by these fierce marauders, but other warm-blooded creatures, such as Seals and the young of the Walrus, also suffer.

In the Northern Pacific great harm is done to the herds of the valuable fur seal when Killers get among them during migration.

The Sperm Whale is safe from their attacks, as he is well able to defend himself with his powerful jaws.

Some authorities have considered that there are several species of the genus *Orca*, but whether this is correct is at present uncertain.

Genus GLOBICEPHALUS

The Pilot Whale or Black-fish
Globicephalus melas, Traill
pl. 48 **bottom**

The Pilot Whale, Ca'ing Whale, or Black-fish as it is variously named, measures from 16 to 24 feet in length. The head is short, and characterised by a high bulging forehead. There is no beak, but the upper jaw projects slightly over the lower.

The jaws contain ten or eleven pairs of teeth in each, though the number is often less in aged animals. The line of the mouth is oblique.

The skin is very smooth and shiny, and has been compared to oiled silk.

The colour in general is bluish black, with a white line extending along the belly, which expands into a broad heart-shaped marking on the throat. The dorsal fin is low, the flippers long, narrow, and curved.

Whales the same or allied to this species are found widely distributed over the oceans of the world. They are plentiful in the North Atlantic, ranging as far north as Greenland, while in the Pacific they are abundant around the coasts of Australia and New Zealand.

In British waters it is chiefly found about the Shetlands, Orkneys, and Western Isles of Scotland, less frequently in England, where it is stranded from time to time on the coasts, a 'school' having come ashore in Mount's Bay, Cornwall, in the summer of 1911.

The Pilot Whale is very gregarious, and often to be seen in large herds containing hundreds of individuals, which appear to be under control of an experienced leader whom they will blindly follow even to their death. This trait in their character is taken advantage of by the Shetlanders and other islanders, who by watching the approach of a herd as it enters some sound or bay, organise great drives of the animals, and cutting them off from the sea, cause large numbers to run aground. They are then stabbed and done to death while struggling helplessly in shallow water.

This method of taking the Pilot Whale goes back for centuries, an old Danish writer of the seventeenth century having recorded about a thousand of these animals in two places in the Faroes in 1664.

In Quendale Bay, Shetland, fifteen hundred and forty were killed in about two hours on September 22, 1845, and many others since.

This species owes its Shetland name of 'Ca'ing' Whale or 'Driving Whale' to its habit of blindly and persistently following its leader.

It chiefly feeds on cuttlefish, but various fishes are also eaten.

The oil and flesh are of some value; according to Harvie-Brown and Buckley (*A Fauna of the Orkney Islands*) one hundred and ninety-five Pilot Whales taken near Flotta in the Orkneys were sold for £500 12s. 6d.

Pl. 48.

Killer.
Pilot Whale.

Plate 49

Genus PHOCAENA

The Common Porpoise
Phocaena communis, Cuvier
pl. 49 **top**

The Common Porpoise, the smallest and most abundant of British Cetaceans, usually measures from 4 to 5 feet and occasionally more in length. The head is rounded and has no external beak. Each jaw is furnished with about twenty-five teeth, which are spade-shaped and not conical as in many of this group. The triangular dorsal fin is placed about the middle of the back.

The colour of the upper parts is a glossy greyish black, which is more or less blended into the white of the throat and belly. The Porpoise is a common species on both sides of the Atlantic, keeping mostly near the coasts. It is abundant all round the British shores and the Atlantic Coasts of France as well as those of Northern Europe, but rarely occurs in the Mediterranean. It goes as far north as Baffin's Bay and southwards to the North American coast.

The Porpoise is also found in the Pacific on the western side of America.

These animals are very sociable, moving about in 'schools', when their black triangular dorsal fins and backs may often be seen above the surface of the water as they follow and play around a vessel at sea, or swim with an easy-going rolling motion among the waters close inshore.

In their playful moods, they will leap quite clear of the sea, as shown in the Plate. They seem to have no dislike to fresh water and will ascend rivers like the Thames where they have been seen well above London Bridge.

The Porpoise lives chiefly on fish, including grilse, mackerel, herring, pilchard, and others, and will often follow the shoals as they approach the coast.

At one time its flesh was popular as an article of food.

Genus GRAMPUS

Risso's Grampus
Grampus griseus, Cuvier
pl. 49 **centre**

Closely related to the Pilot Whale, Risso's Grampus differs in the contour of the head which is less rounded, in the small number of teeth confined to the front part of the lower jaw, and also in possessing a high and falcated dorsal fin. The scimitar-shaped flippers are rather long, but shorter than those of the Pilot Whale.

In the *Transactions of the Zoological Society* (vol. viii. pp. 3–13), Sir William Flower has given an account of this rare species taken from a freshly killed specimen caught in a mackerel-net off the Eddystone lighthouse on February 28th, 1870, with a carefully coloured drawing of the animal. By kind permission of the Publication Committee I have copied this for the figure in Plate 49, and the following notes are taken from the description:

'The most prevalent tint was grey varying in some parts to pure white and in others to deep black, but the light parts of the head and anterior portion of the body had a yellowish wash, and the dark parts a slightly bluish or purple tinge which varied much in different lights.

'The head and the whole of the anterior to the dorsal fin was generally a lighter grey, variegated with patches of both darker and lighter hue. The eye was surrounded by a small oval patch of black. The lips were mottled with black. There was a large nearly black patch on the top of the head, extending backwards a short distance behind the blow-hole, and on each side towards but not reaching the eye. Both surfaces of the pectoral fin were nearly black, very finely mottled or dappled with grey, and becoming darker towards the tip.

'The neighbourhood of the axilla was of the same dappled colour. . . . But what gave the most remarkable and characteristic appearance to the animal was the presence of conspicuous, but most irregular, light streaks and spots scattered over the whole of the side from the front of the head to about two feet from the end of the tail, where they ceased, at least on the lateral surface. . . . The streaks or lines were of various lengths and running in all directions in a most fantastic manner, some parallel, some crossing each other, and some forming sharp angles, zigzags and scribble-like patterns.'

The total length of this specimen was 10 feet 6 inches.

Risso's Grampus has a very extensive range, occurring in the Atlantic and Pacific Oceans, and occasionally in some numbers in the Mediterranean. It is rare in British waters. In England the first known example was stranded at Puckaster, Isle of Wight, in the spring of 1843, and a few others have been taken from time to time.

In Scotland, six were captured at Hillswick, Shetland, in September 1889. Two more were stranded on the Solway in 1892 and one in the Forth near Kincardine in October 1904 (Millais). Little seems to be known of the habits of this Dolphin. Judging by the remains of cuttlefish found in captured specimens and the curious marks and scratches on the skin of the animal caused by their beaks and suckers, it appears to feed chiefly on those creatures.

Genus LAGENORHYNCHUS

The White-sided Dolphin
Lagenorhynchus acutus, Gray
pl. 49 **bottom**

Two species of this genus (the Short-beaked Dolphins) characterised by their rounded heads, short beaks, and large number of vertebrae, occur occasionally in the British Islands.

The White-sided Dolphin attains a length of 6 to 8 feet when fully grown, the males being larger than the females. The dorsal fin is high and falcate, the flippers pointed and scimitar-shaped. The body is compact and stout, but much compressed where it joins the flukes of the tail.

My friend Mr Pycraft has kindly supplied me with some notes and sketches taken from freshly killed specimens received at the British Museum of Natural History, from which, with the help of a cast of the animal in the Gallery, I have drawn the figure in the Plate and described the colour.

According to Mr Pycraft, the 'beak and upper surface of the head are dull black, edge of upper jaw (the "tip") shading into dull greyish white towards the gape. A broad belt of black encircles the eye, and from this there runs forward a narrow black line to terminate at about the posterior one-third of the rostral groove.

'Below this line, the white of the flanks and side of the head runs forward to form a narrow wedge interrupted in front of the eye by a band of grey. Above the line and extending backwards in a rapidly widening triangle which includes the black eye patch, the skin is lead coloured. A narrow black line extending backwards to the ear and from the level of the posterior cankus, forming a conspicuous relief to the lead-coloured area.'

The colour of the upper parts of the body is black, broken up by a band of white on the sides which blends into another patch of pale brownish buff extending towards the tail. The throat and belly are white with black markings surrounding the vent. The flippers are black, with a stripe of the same colour extending from their base to the corner of the mouth.

The White-sided Dolphin inhabits the North Atlantic; ranging from as far north as Greenland to the British Islands. It is also found along the eastern shores of the United States.

Dr Gray first described the species from a skull found in the Orkneys, and an adult female was also obtained there in May 1835. A party of about twenty were taken together in Scapa Bay, Kirkwall, on May 21, 1858. One has been recorded from Ardrishaig and another at Dunrobin stranded in April 1906.

A few have been taken in Ireland, one as late as 1916 on the coast of Mayo. Like other Dolphins, this species moves about in 'schools', frequently leaping clear of the water as it sports among the waves along with its companions.

Pl. 49.

Porpoise. 1/5

Risso's Grampus. 1/7
(after Flower) Trans. Zool. Soc.

White-sided Dolphin. 1/5

Plate 50

The White-beaked Dolphin
Lagenorhynchus albirostris, Gray
pl. 50 **top**

The White-beaked Dolphin measures from 7 to about 9½ feet in length. The creamy-white beak is well pronounced and very distinct, in contrast to the dark frontal portion of the head. The jaws contain about twenty-six pairs of small sharp teeth in each.

The dorsal fin is large and curved.

In colour, the upper parts of the head and body are purplish black, the beak, lips, throat, and underparts creamy white.

The lips are often marked with spots of grey, and mottled patches also occur on the sides of the shoulders and on the back.

Like the White-sided Dolphin this species inhabits the North Atlantic, frequenting Davis Straits, the seas of Greenland, and across to Scandinavia and the British Islands, where examples have been stranded from time to time on the coasts. Its habits, as far as we know, do not appear to differ from those of other Dolphins.

Genus DELPHINUS

The Common Dolphin
Delphinus delphis, Linnaeus
pl. 50 **bottom**

In this genus, of which the Common Dolphin is the type, the elongated snout takes the form of a distinct beak. The mouth of the Common Dolphin contains from forty to sixty pairs of small sharp teeth in each jaw, the dorsal fin is large, and like the flippers, is more or less sickle-shaped in outline.

The body is long and very graceful in its lines, measuring from beak to tail from 6 to 8 feet long.

Sir William Flower thus describes its varied colouring from a specimen captured off the coast of Cornwall in March 1879 (*Transactions Zoological Society*, vol. xi. p. 2): 'Instead of being simply black above and white below, as usually described, the sides were shaded, mottled, and streaked with various tints of yellow and grey. . . . The under surface was of the purest possible white.'

The figure on Plate 50 has been drawn from the coloured picture of this specimen illustrating Sir William Flower's paper, by kind permission of the Publication Committee.

According to Millais, the underparts of the Common Dolphin are, in early winter, grey or greenish white.

It inhabits the temperate parts of the Atlantic, and similar or closely related forms are found in the Pacific.

It is common in the Bay of Biscay, and also in the Mediterranean, where it was well known to the ancient Greeks, who were fond of representing its elegant outlines on their coins.

In the British Islands it often appears off the coast of Cornwall and in the Channel, when it sometimes gets entangled in the fishermen's nets. Though rare in Scotland, it has been captured both on the eastern and western coasts and also in the Shetlands.

It is extremely sociable in its habits and may often be seen in the Mediterranean and other favourite waters, as it plays in large shoals around vessels, leaping out of the sea and showing wonderful agility and gracefulness.

The food consists of various fishes, including herrings and mackerel; cuttlefish and crustaceans are also eaten.

The mother Dolphin shows great affection for her single young one, which is carefully nursed and tended.

The flesh was at one time much sought after as an article of food, especially in France, and like the meat of other cetaceans was looked upon as fish and allowed to be eaten on fast days.

The Bottle-nosed Dolphin
Tursiops tursio, Fabricius
pl. 50 **centre**

Apart from colour and size, the chief external difference between this species and its near relation the Common Dolphin, lies in the shape of the beak, which in the Bottle-nosed Dolphin is short and depressed and has the lower jaw slightly longer than the upper. It has also fewer teeth, possessing only from twenty to twenty-five pairs in each jaw.

The total length of the animal is from 8 to 10 feet.

The colour of the upper part of the head and body, including the fins and tail, is a glossy purplish or greyish black, the margin of the upper lip to the point of the beak, greyish white, the lower jaw, throat and belly, white. In some individuals the colour of the underparts is dark grey marked with patches of white.

This Dolphin is not uncommon off the coasts on either side of the Atlantic, in America ranging as far south as the Gulf of Mexico, and in Europe occurring in the North Sea, Bay of Biscay, and Mediterranean (Millais). A good many have been captured on the English coasts, the first recorded having been a female taken along with a sucker near Berkeley, and described by John Hunter in 1787.

Its occurrence in Northern Britain seems to be less frequent, though it appears from time to time along the Scottish shores. In October 1901 a party of six were stranded at Inverness.

It has seldom been recorded in Ireland.

There is no evidence to show that it differs much from the Common Dolphin in its actions or habits.

Pl. 50.

White-beaked Dolphin.

Bottle-nosed Dolphin.

Common Dolphin.

Appendix
by Iain Bishop

Mammals Extinct in the British Islands Within Historic Times

Mammals described by Thorburn in this section (an Appendix in the original edition) but not illustrated are:

Canis lupus Linnaeus, 1758 The Wolf

Ursus arctos Linnaeus, 1758 The Brown Bear

Castor fiber Linnaeus, 1758 The Beaver

Rangifer tarandus (Linnaeus, 1758) The Reindeer
A small domesticated herd of this species was re-introduced in the Cairngorms, Scotland, in 1952.

Sus scrofa Linnaeus, 1758 The Wild Boar

Plate 1
Order CHEIROPTERA

This name is now more usually spelled CHIROPTERA. The British list now includes thirteen indigenous species plus two vagrant (non-breeding species), as follows.

Family RHINOLOPHIDAE

Rhinolophus ferrumequinum (Schreber, 1774) The Greater Horse-shoe Bat
A recent paper by Racey and Stebbings (1972), describing a survey of the status of bat colonies in Britain, notes a considerable decline in the range of the Greater Horse-shoe Bat (see also Corbet, 1971) and in the size of its population.

Rhinolophus hipposideros (Bechstein, 1800) The Lesser Horse-shoe Bat

Plate 2
Family VESPERTILIONIDAE

Barbastella barbastellus (Schreber, 1774) The Barbastelle
Its near ally mentioned by Thorburn, *B. darjilingensis* (now called *B. leucomelas*) is widely distributed in Asia.

Plecotus auritus (Linnaeus, 1758) The Long-eared Bat
Stebbings (1967) has shown that two species of *Plecotus* can be distinguished in Britain. *P. auritus*, the Common Long-eared Bat, is the smaller of the two and has a more northerly distribution. *P. austriacus* (Fischer, 1829), the Grey Long-eared Bat, is somewhat larger and its range is restricted to some southern counties (Dorset, Hampshire) and Jersey. The distribu-

tion of these two species overlaps on the Continent of Europe. In England the Grey Long-eared Bat is now known from only one roost.

Plate 3
Genus *Vesperugo*
Now known as *Eptesicus*.

Vesperugo noctula The Noctule or Great Bat
Now known as *Nyctalus noctula* (Schreber, 1774).

Pipistrellus pipistrellus (Schreber, 1774) The Pipistrelle or Common Bat

Plate 4
Vesperugo serotinus The Serotine
Now known as *Eptesicus serotinus* (Schreber, 1774).

Vespertilio murinus (Linnaeus, 1758) The Parti-coloured Bat
Now regarded as a 'vagrant'; an occasional visitor not breeding in the British Isles.

Vesperugo leisleri Leisler's Bat
Now known as *Nyctalus leisleri* (Kuhl, 1818); also called the Lesser Noctule.

Plate 5
Genus *Myotis*
Myotis daubentoni (Kuhl, 1819) Daubenton's Bat

Myotis nattereri (Kuhl, 1818) Natterer's Bat

Plate 6
Myotis mystacinus (Kuhl, 1819) Whiskered Bat

Myotis bechsteini (Kuhl, 1818) Bechstein's Bat

Myotis myotis (Borkhausen, 1797) The Mouse-eared Bat
This species is not recorded by Thorburn. It is the largest British species, with a wingspan of up to 450 mm (more usually in the range of 350–410 mm). The forearm usually measures over 58 mm. It is a tricoloured bat with clear demarkation between the brown back and grey-white belly. This species was known to inhabit several roosts in Dorset in the 1950s, but declined because of disturbance and has been recently rediscovered as a single colony in Sussex (Phillips and Blackmore, 1970). The numbers of this bat are declining all through Europe and its normally precarious hold in England is now very tenuous.

Plate 7
Order INSECTIVORA
Erinaceus europaeus Linnaeus, 1758 The Hedgehog

Plate 8
Talpa europaea Linnaeus, 1758 The Common Mole

Plate 9
Sorex araneus Linnaeus, 1758 The Common Shrew

The British race of *S. araneus* is considered to be sufficiently distinct to warrant the subspecific name *castaneus* Jenyns, 1838. On the island of Jersey a race known as *S. a. fretalis* Miller, 1909, is found; on Islay *S. a. granti* Barrett-Hamilton and Hinton, 1913, is named as a separate subspecies.

Sorex minutus Linnaeus, 1766 The Lesser or Pigmy Shrew

Neomys fodiens Pennant, 1771 The Water Shrew Thorburn seems to have ignored the white-toothed shrews of the Channel Islands and Scillies. These have never been found on the mainland of Britain but are represented on the Continent of Europe. *Crocidura russula* (Hermann, 1780) is found on Guernsey, Alderney and Herm. *C. suaveolens* (Pallas, 1811) is found on Jersey and Sark and, being a smaller animal, is known as the Lesser White-toothed Shrew. A slightly different form is encountered on the Scilly Islands. This has been given the name *C. suaveolens cassiteridum* Hinton, 1924. White-toothed shrews, while similar in general form to other British species, do not possess the red pigmentation on the teeth which is found in *Sorex* and *Neomys*.

Plate 10

Order CARNIVORA

Felis catus The Wild Cat

Now known as *F. silvestris* Schreber, 1777. The Scottish race is considered to be distinct and named *F. s. grampia* Miller, 1907.

Plate 11

Canis vulpes The Fox

Now known as *Vulpes vulpes* (Linnaeus, 1758).

Plate 12

PINNIPEDIA is now regarded as a full Order.

Trichechus rosmarus The Walrus

Now known as *Odobenus rosmarus* (Linnaeus, 1758). This is a vagrant species, not breeding in the British Isles.

Plate 13

Halichoerus grypus (Fabricius, 1791) The Grey Seal

Plate 14

Phoca vitulina Linnaeus, 1758 The Common Seal

Plate 15

Phoca hispida Schreber, 1775 The Ringed Seal This is a vagrant species, not breeding in the British Isles.

Phoca groenlandica Erxleben, 1777 The Harp or Greenland Seal

This is also a vagrant species.

Plate 16

Erignathus barbatus (Erxleben, 1777) The Bearded Seal

A vagrant species.

Cystophora cristata (Erxleben, 1777) The Hooded Seal

A vagrant species.

Plate 17

Family MUSTELIDAE

Lutra vulgaris The Common Otter

Now known as *L. lutra* (Linnaeus, 1758).

Plate 18

Meles taxus The Badger

Now known as *M. meles* (Linnaeus, 1758).

Plate 19

Mustela martes The Pine Marten

Now known as *Martes martes* (Linnaeus, 1758).

Plate 20

Mustela putorius Linnaeus, 1758 The Polecat

Plates 21 and 22

Mustela erminea Linnaeus, 1758 The Stoat

This species possibly includes two geographical races, *M. e. hibernica* Thomas and Barrett-Hamilton, 1895, from Ireland, and *M. e. ricinae* Miller, 1907, from Islay and Jura.

Plate 23

Mustela vulgaris The Weasel

Now known as *M. nivalis* Linnaeus, 1766.

Mustela vison Schreber, 1777 The American Mink

The American Mink is a medium-sized mustelid about 18 inches to 2 feet long with a short (5 to 9-inch) tail. Males are somewhat larger than females. The pelt is a rich dark brown in colour all over, though occasionally some white belly markings are found. A white spot is present on the chin.

The mink appears to be a cunning and determined escaper. It has been living wild since the early 1930s when the first mink farms were established in Britain. Strict security arrangements are now made to minimise the risks of further escapes.

The mink now breeds in suitable habitats almost throughout Britain from north-east Scotland to Wales, Devon and Hampshire. The banks of streams, rivers and lakes are its favoured sites and it is an excellent swimmer. The bulk of its diet in Britain is fish, though it makes occasional raids on poultry. This species has proved difficult to control, but is being studied intensively to evaluate its effects as a pest.

Order RODENTIA

Family CAPROMYIDAE

Myocastor coypus (Molina, 1782) The Coypu

The Coypu (famous for its fur which, when guard hairs have been removed, is known as '*nutria*') was introduced from South America. It became feral in East Anglia from 1929, when the first farm was established, especially in the Norfolk Broads.

The Coypu is a large water-loving rat with webbed feet. The length of head and body combined may reach nearly 2 feet and its tail up to 1 foot. In general colour it is dark brown or blackish with a grey belly. The Coypu lives in reed beds, marshes and river banks. It has been known to damage crops and to destroy the reed-beds used in thatching. Intensive efforts to reduce the population have met with some success, but it has not been exterminated.

Family CRICETIDAE

Ondatra zibethicus (Molina, 1782) The Musk Rat

The Musk Rat was introduced in the 1930s for fur farming. It escaped several times but, after an intensive campaign to destroy it, it is now believed to have been exterminated.

Family SCIURIDAE

Sciurus vulgaris Linnaeus, 1758 The Common Squirrel

The British race is considered by some to be sufficiently different from its Continental neighbours to be given the subspecific name *Sciurus vulgaris leucourus* Kerr, 1792.

Sciurus carolinensis Gmelin, 1788 The American Grey Squirrel

The American Grey Squirrel, as its name suggests, is usually easily distinguished from the native Red Squirrel by colour. However, in its summer coat, which is brownish and has a rufous streak along the flanks and on the paws, some confusion may arise. The Red Squirrel can be distinguished by its characteristic ear tufts. The Grey Squirrel has been introduced to Britain several times since the late nineteenth century and is now found in most of England, Wales, some southern Scottish counties, and in many localities in Ireland. The distribution is determined by the presence of mixed deciduous woodland or woodland with about 25 per cent hardwoods. It can live in coniferous forests only if some deciduous woodland exists near by.

This species is regarded as a pest, particularly by foresters, whose plantations of young trees may be severely damaged by bark stripping. At present control is difficult and strict government regulations control its importation and keeping.

Plate 25

Muscardinus avellanarius (Linnaeus, 1758) The Common Dormouse

Family GLIRIDAE

Glis glis (Linnaeus, 1766) The Edible or Fat Dormouse

The Edible Dormouse is a large dormouse, about a foot from nose to tail tip, with a long bushy tail. It is found only in the Hertfordshire, Buckinghamshire and Bedfordshire areas. It was introduced at Tring, Herts, in 1902.

The dormouse is grey-brown in colour with dark stripes on the outsides of its legs and a dark ring around its eyes. It hibernates in winter and may invade houses in autumn in search of a sheltered spot for the winter. Its summer habitat is deciduous woodland. It is nocturnal and almost completely arboreal.

In Roman times *Glis* was fattened and eaten as a delicacy.

Plate 26

Genus *Micromys*

Mus minutus The Harvest Mouse

Now known as *Micromys minutus* (Pallas, 1771).

Mus sylvaticus The Wood Mouse

Now known as *Apodemus sylvaticus* (Linnaeus, 1758)

Plate 27

Mus sylvaticus wintoni The British Yellow-necked Wood Mouse

Now known as *Apodemus flavicollis* (Melchior, 1834).

Mus sylvaticus hirtensis The St Kilda Field Mouse

Now known as *Apodemus sylvaticus hirtensis* Barrett-Hamilton, 1899.

Mus sylvaticus hebridensis The Hebridean Field Mouse

Now known as *Apodemus sylvaticus hebridensis* (de Winton, 1895).

Mus sylvaticus celticus The Irish Wood Mouse

Now known as *Apodemus sylvaticus celticus* Barrett-Hamilton, 1900. This latter race is not now considered sufficiently different from the mainland *A. sylvaticus* to warrant subspecific distinction.

At various times almost every island form has been given a separate subspecific name, most of which are no longer regarded as valid.

Plate 28

Mus musculus Linnaeus, 1758 The Common or House Mouse

Mus occurs on several islands round Britain and the island specimens tend to be larger than those of the mainland. Largely on the basis of large size, two subspecies were named, *M. m. faeroensis* Clarke, 1904, from the Faeroes, and *M. m. muralis* Barrett-Hamilton, 1899 (now extinct) from St Kilda.

Plate 29

Mus rattus The Black Rat

Now known as *Rattus rattus* (Linnaeus, 1758).

Thorburn also refers to *Mus decumanus*, which is now known as *Rattus norvegicus*, and to *Mus alexandrinus*, the Alexandrine Rat, now known as *Rattus rattus alexandrinus*.

The true *R. rattus* coloration is black above and grey below. Other colour variations of this species found in Britain have been named as subspecies – *R. r. alexandrinus* (Geoffroy, 1803) and *R. r. frugivorous* (Rafinesque, 1814) – but probably do not deserve this status.

Plate 30

Mus decumanus The Brown Rat

Now known as *Rattus norvegicus* (Berkenhout, 1769).

Plate 31

Evotomys glareolus The Bank Vole

Now known as *Clethrionomys glareolus* (Schreber, 1780).

Evotomys hercynicus Skomerensis The Skomer Vole

Now known as *Clethrionomys glareolus skomerensis* (Barrett-Hamilton, 1904).

Evotomys alstoni The Mull Vole

Now known as *Clethrionomys glareolus alstoni* (Barrett-Hamilton and Hinton, 1913).

Evotomys erica The Raasay Vole

Now known as *Clethrionomys glareolus erica* (Barrett-Hamilton and Hinton, 1913).

These are all now regarded as subspecies of the mainland form. Except for a reference in his quotation from Barrett-Hamilton, Thorburn does not mention the Jersey subspecies *C. g. caesarius* (Miller, 1908).

Microtus agrestis (Linnaeus, 1761) The Common Field Vole

Subspecies have been named from various Hebridean Islands: *M. a. mial* Barrett-Hamilton and Hinton, 1913, from Eigg; *M. a. luch* Barrett-Hamilton and Hinton, 1913, from Muck; *M. a. macgillivrayi* Barrett-Hamilton and Hinton, 1913, from Islay; and *M. a. fiona* Montagu, 1922, from Gigha.

Microtus orcadensis The Orkney Vole

Now known as *M. arvalis* (Pallas, 1779). The similarities of the Orkney voles to *M. arvalis* of the Continent and the fact that they interbreed freely with that species suggest that they should belong to it. Several names have been suggested for the various island populations, *M. a. orcadensis* Millais, 1904, on the mainland of Orkney; *M. a. sandayensis*, Millais, 1905, on Sanday and Westray; *M. a. ronaldshaiensis* Hinton, 1913, on Ronsay Island.

The Jersey Vole also belongs to this species and has been named *M. a. sarnius* Miller, 1909.

Plate 32

Sub-Genus *Arvicola*

Arvicola is usually regarded as having full generic status.

Arvicola amphibius The Water Vole

Now known as *A. terrestris* (Linnaeus, 1758).

Plate 33

Group or Sub-Order DUPLICIDENTATA

Now replaced by Order LAGOMORPHA.

Lepus europaeus The Common Hare

Now known as *L. capensis* Linnaeus, 1758. Recently Petter (1961) has suggested that the European and some African hares are conspecific. The name *L. capensis* which is applied to the relevant group of African hares thus comes to apply to both as it antedates *L. europaeus* Pallas, 1778.

Plates 34 and 35

Lepus timidus Linnaeus, 1758 The Mountain Hare

The Irish and Scottish races of *L. timidus* are considered by some taxonomists subspecifically different and are called *L. t. hibernicus* Bell, 1837 and *L. t. scoticus* Hilzheimer, 1906 respectively.

Plate 36

Lepus cuniculus The Rabbit or Cony

Now known as *Oryctolagus cuniculus* (Linnaeus, 1758).

Plate 37

Order RUMINANTIA

Now known as Order ARTIODACTYLA.

Family CERVIDAE

Cervus elaphus Linnaeus, 1758 The Red Deer

The British race is known as *C. e. scoticus* Lönneberg, 1906.

Plate 38

Cervus dama The Fallow Deer

Now known as *Dama dama* (Linnaeus, 1758).

Plate 39

Capreolus capreolus (Linnaeus, 1758) The Roe Deer

Several other species of deer have been introduced to Britain at various times including the Sika, *Cervus nippon* Temminck, 1838, the Indian Muntjac, *Muntiacus muntjak* (Zimmerman, 1780), the Chinese Muntjac, *M. reevesi* (Ogilby, 1839) and the Chinese Water Deer, *Hydropotes inermis* Swinhoe, 1870. The Reindeer, *Rangifer tarandus* (Linnaeus, 1758), was once native, became extinct and has recently been reintroduced in Scotland under domestication.

Cervus nippon Temminck, 1838 The Sika Deer
The Sika Deer is in appearance a smaller version of the Red Deer, standing only 3 feet high at the shoulder, and has simplified antlers which may measure up to 25 inches in length. The antlers are in velvet during early summer (May to July), are fully cleaned by September and cast in early April.

Introduced to deer parks during the mid-nineteenth century, the Sika has escaped several times and can now be found in wet thickets and mixed woodland in many counties of England, Scotland and Ireland.

The Sika lies up during the day and forages from dusk to dawn, eating herbs and grass. It occasionally damages trees and crops.

Muntiacus reevesi (Ogilby, 1839) The Chinese Muntjac
Although both *M. reevesi*, the Chinese Muntjac, and *M. muntjak*, the Indian Muntjac, have been introduced at various times to deer parks, only the former appears to have successfully adapted to feral life in Britain. It is now a widespread species in thick woodland in the Home Counties and the Midlands. The Muntjac is a small species standing only 17 inches at the shoulder. The upper canine teeth are developed as short, curved tusks in male specimens, antlers are small and simple with only a single brow tine. Females have no antlers but a pair of tufts of black hair in their place. Its general colour is a deep red, with darker colour on the back of the ears.

The Muntjac eats mainly shrubs, fruits, grass and roots and has been known to damage a number of crops. This species appears to be relatively unsuited to the worst extremes of the British climate and many individuals die in severe winters.

Hydropotes inermis Swinhoe, 1870 The Chinese Water Deer
The Chinese Water Deer is very limited in distribution. It was introduced at Woburn, Bedfordshire, at the beginning of the twentieth century and can now be found in woodland and grassland in the counties of Bedfordshire, Hertfordshire and Buckinghamshire. From separate introductions it has now become feral in a limited area of north Hampshire and Shropshire.

The Water Deer is a small species, measuring only 20 inches at the shoulder. The white markings round the nose, eyes, lower jaw and inner parts of the ear stand out against the general buff of the head and ears. The coat is of pale chestnut with black stippling and becomes darker in winter. Males and females are similar.
Plates 40 and 41

Bos taurus Wild White Cattle
Now regarded as *Bos* (domestic). These 'wild' white cattle are thought to be descended from the urus *B. premigenius* Bojanus, 1827, and exist as herds maintained in parks.
Plate 42

Order CETACEA
Family BALAENIDAE
Balaena australis The Greenland or Arctic Right Whale
Now known as *B. glacialis* (Borowski, 1781).
Family BALAENOPTERIDAE
Megaptera boöps The Humpbacked Whale
Now known as *M. novaeangliae* (Borowski, 1781).
Plate 43

Balaenoptera sibbaldii Sibbald's Rorqual or Blue Whale
Now known as *B. musculus* (Linnaeus, 1758).
Balaenoptera musculus The Common Rorqual
Now known as *B. physalus* (Linnaeus, 1758).
Plate 44

Balaenoptera borealis Lesson, 1828 Rudolphi's Rorqual
Balaenoptera acutorostrata (Lacépède, 1804) The Lesser Rorqual
Family ZIPHIIDAE
Hyperoödon rostratum The Bottle-nosed Whale
Now known as *H. ampullatus* (Forster, 1770). Also shown in Plate 45.
Plate 45

Family PHYSETERIDAE
Physeter macrocephalus The Sperm Whale or Cachalot
Now known as *P. catodon* Linnaeus, 1758.
Plate 46

Family ZIPHIIDAE
Ziphius cavirostris G. Cuvier, 1823 Cuvier's Whale
Mesoplodon bidens (Sowerby, 1804) Sowerby's Whale

Mesoplodon mirus True, 1913 True's Beaked Whale

Plate 47

Family MONODONTIDAE

Monodon monoceros Linnaeus, 1758 The Narwhal

Delphinapterus leucas (Pallas, 1776) The White Whale or Beluga

Plate 48

Family DELPHINIDAE

Orca gladiator The Killer or Grampus

Now known as *Orcinus orca* (Linnaeus, 1758).

Globicephalus melas The Pilot Whale or Black-fish

Now known as *Globicephala melaena* (Traill, 1809).

Plate 49

Family PHOCOENIDAE

Phocaena communis The Common Porpoise

Now known as *Phocoena phocoena* (Linnaeus, 1758).

Family DELPHINIDAE

Grampus griseus (Cuvier, 1812) Risso's Grampus

Lagenorhynchus acutus (Gray, 1828) The White-sided Dolphin

Plate 50

Lagenorhynchus albirostris Gray, 1846 The White-beaked Dolphin

Delphinus delphis Linnaeus, 1758 The Common Dolphin

Tursiops tursio The Bottle-nosed Dolphin

Now known as *T. truncatus* (Montagu, 1821).

The Bottle-nosed Dolphin
[tail-piece from page 99 of the 1920–1 edition]

Bibliographical Note

The order in which species are discussed in the 1920–1 text has been slightly rearranged so that each species description appears on the page opposite the relevant plate. These changes are shown below. Roman numerals refer to the original two volumes.

Books Illustrated by Archibald Thorburn's Plates

In the following alphabetical-by-author list of books illustrated by Thorburn, and of some later books in which his plates have been reproduced, the year or years cited are those of the first edition unless otherwise indicated.

Anker, Jean, *Bird Books and Bird Art: An Outline of the History and Iconography of Descriptive Ornithology*. Levin and Munksgaard, Copenhagen, 1938.

Archer, Sir Geoffrey Francis and Godman, Eva Mary, *The Birds of British Somaliland and the Gulf of Aden*. Gurney & Jackson, London, 1937 (vols 1 and 2); Oliver & Boyd, London, 1937 (vols 3 and 4). Contains Thorburn's last published plates.

Beebe, C. W., *A Monograph of the Pheasants*. Witherby, London; 4 vols, 1918–22. Some of the finest of the 90 colour plates are by Thorburn.

Benson, S. Vere, *The Observer's Book of British Birds*. Warne, London, 1937. Contains many Thorburn plates from Lilford (1885–98).

Brander, Michael (Ed.), *The International Encyclopedia of Shooting*. Pelham, London, 1972. Contains a Thorburn plate of blackcock.

Buxton, Sydney Charles [Earl Buxton], *Fishing and Shooting*. John Murray, London, 1902.

Coward, T. A., *The Birds of the British Isles and Their Eggs*. Warne, London, 1920–6; 3 vols. Contains many Thorburn plates from Lilford (1885–98).

Coward, T. A., *Bird Haunts and Nature Memories*. Warne, London, 1922. Contains a fine Thorburn frontispiece of a noctule, dated 10 October 1919.

Coward, T. A., *Bird Life At Home and Abroad with Other Nature Observations*. Warne, London and New York, 1927.

Dale, Thomas Francis, *The Fox*. Longmans, Green & Co., London, 1906 (*Fur, Feather and Fin Series, no. 12*).

Dewar, George Albermarle Bertie, *Life and Sport in Hampshire*. Longmans, Green & Co., London, 1908. Includes two colour plates by Thorburn.

Dresser, Henry Eeles, Sharpe, Richard Bowdler and Hay, Arthur Viscount Walden, *A History of the Birds in Europe, Including all the Species Inhabiting the Western Palaearctic Region*. Published by the author, London; 9 vols including supplement, originally published in 93 parts 1871–81, 1895–6.

[Drewitt, C. M.,] *Lord Lilford . . . A Memoir by His Sister* [Hon. Mrs F. Dawtrey Drewitt]. Smith Elder, London, 1900. Includes seven plates in monochrome by Thorburn of Lilford Hall, Northamptonshire, and living birds in its aviaries.

Fisher, James, *Thorburn's Birds*. Michael Joseph, London, 1967. Includes 82 plates from Thorburn (1915–16).

Gladstone, H. S., *Handbook to Lord Lilford's Coloured Figures of the Birds of the British Islands*. Bickers, London, 1917.

Grimble, Augustus, *The Deer Forests of Scotland*. Kegan Paul & Co., London, 1896. Eight monochrome illustrations are by Thorburn.

Grimble, Augustus, *Deer-Stalking and the Deer Forests of Scotland*. Kegan Paul & Co., London, 1901. Eight monochrome illustrations are by Thorburn.

Grimble, Augustus, *Highland Sport*. Chapman & Hall, London, 1894.

Grimble, Augustus, *The Salmon Rivers of Scotland*. Kegan Paul & Co., London, 1902.

Grimble, Augustus, *Shooting and Salmon Fishing and Highland Sport*. Kegan Paul & Co., London, 1902. Contains 16 monochrome illustrations by Thorburn.

Hardy [Gathorne-Hardy], Hon. Alfred Erskine, *Autumns in Argyleshire with Rod and Gun*. Longmans, Green & Co., London, 1900.

Harting, James Edmund, *Sketches of Bird Life*. Allen & Co., London, 1883. Two monochrome plates are by Thorburn, the first of his to be published.

Harting, James Edmund, *The Rabbit*. Longmans, Green & Co., London, 1898 (*Fur, Feather and Fin Series*, no. 6). Monochrome frontispiece is by Thorburn.

Hudson, William Henry, and Beddard, Frank E., *British Birds*. Longmans, Green & Co., London, 1895. Eight coloured plates are by Thorburn.

Irby, L. Howard L., *The Ornithology of the Straits of Gibraltar*. Porter, London, 2nd ed. 1895. Eight colour plates are by Thorburn.

Koenig, A. [F.], *Avifauna Spitzbergensis. . . .* Published by the author, Bonn, 1911. Colour frontispiece of little auks was painted by Thorburn in 1910.

Lakatos, Károly, *A Vadászmesterseg Könyve*. Budapest, 1903.

Lilford, Baron [Thomas Little Powys], *Coloured Figures of the Birds of the British Islands*. Porter, London, 1885–98; 36 parts in 7 vols. Thorburn was brought in to the work of illustration in January 1887 and his first plate was published in part 7, vol. 2 in September 1888. He finally did the bulk of the work, 268 colour plates of the total of 421.

Lilford, Baron [Thomas Littleton Powys], *Notes on the Birds of Northamptonshire and Neighbourhood*. Porter, London, 1895; 2 vols. Contains 24 monochrome plates of birds and Northamptonshire scenery by Thorburn.

Little, Alicia Bewicke [Mrs Archibald], *Our Pet Herons*. Roy. Soc. Protect. Birds Leafl. no. 35. Contains Thorburn monochrome drawing of little egrets.

MacPherson, H. A. and others, *The Partridge*. Longmans, Green & Co., London, 1893 (*Fur and Feather Series*, no. 1). Nine monochrome plates are by Thorburn.

MacPherson, H. A. and others, *The Grouse*. Longmans, Green & Co., London, 1894 (*Fur and Feather Series*, no. 2). Ten monochrome plates and one vignette are by Thorburn.

MacPherson, H. A. and others, *The Pheasant*. Longmans, Green & Co., London, 1894 (*Fur and Feather Series*, no. 3). Nine plates (ten in 2nd edition, 1896) and one vignette, in monochrome, are by Thorburn.

MacPherson, H. A. and others, *The Hare*. Longmans, Green & Co., London, 1896 (*Fur and Feather Series*, no. 4). Three monochrome plates are by Thorburn.

MacPherson, H. A. and others, *The Red Deer*. Longmans, Green & Co., London, 1896 (*Fur and Feather Series*, no. 5). Six monochrome plates are by Thorburn.

Matschie, Paul, *Bilder aus dem Tierleben*. Union, Stuttgart, 1900.

Millais, John Guille, *The Natural History of the British Surface-Feeding Ducks*. Longmans, Green & Co., London, 1902. Eight colour plates are by Thorburn.

Millais, John Guille, *The Mammals of Great Britain and Ireland*. Longmans, Green & Co., London, 1904–6; 3 vols. Contains 30 colour plates by Thorburn done between 1893 and 1905.

Millais, John Guille, *The Natural History of the British Game Birds*. Longmans, Green & Co., London, 1909. Some of the 18 colour plates are by Thorburn.

Millais, John Guille, *British Diving Ducks*. Longmans, Green & Co., London, 1913; 2 vols. Contains 15 colour plates by Thorburn.

Millais, John Guille, *Rhododendrons*. Longmans, Green & Co., London, 1917, 1924; 2 vols. Contains two colour plates by Thorburn.

Millais, John Guille and others, *British Gamebirds and Wildfowl*, London, 1912 (*The Gun at Home and Abroad*); 2 vols. Some of the illustrations are by Thorburn.

Owen, J. A., 'The Lilford Vivaria'. *Pall Mall Mag.* 48–61, September 1896. Contains six monochrome illustrations by Thorburn.

Peek, Hedley, *The Poetry of Sport*. Longmans, Green & Co., London, 1885 (*Badminton Library*). Some of the illustrations are by Thorburn.

Powys, Thomas Littleton see Lilford

Pycraft, W. P., *Birds of Great Britain and Their Natural History*. Williams and Norgate, London, 1934. Colour frontispiece by Thorburn from Hudson and Beddard, 1895.

Shaw, L. H. de Visme and others, *Snipe and Woodcock*. Longmans, Green & Co., London, 1903 (*Fur, Feather and Fin Series*, no. 10). Contains four monochrome plates by Thorburn.

Sitwell, Sacheverell, Buchanan, Handasyde and Fisher, James, *Fine Bird Books 1700–1900*. Collins, London, and Van Nostrand, New York, 1953.

Stewart, Henry Elliott, *The Birds of Our Country*, Digby & Long, London, 1897.

Swaysland, Walter, *Familiar Wild Birds*. Cassell & Co., London, 1883–8; 4 vols. Contains 144 coloured lithographs by Thorburn, his first major publishing assignment.

Trevor-Battye, A. (Ed.), *Lord Lilford on Birds*, Hutchinson & Co., London, 1903.

Thorburn, Archibald, 'Sabine's Gull in Cornwall'. *Zoologist*, 475–6.

Thorburn, Archibald, *British Birds*. Longmans, Green & Co., London, 1915–18; 4 vols. Contains 80 plates in colour, showing over 400 species.

Thorburn, Archibald, *A Naturalist's Sketch Book*. Longmans, Green & Co., London, 1919. Contains 60 plates, 24 in colour.

Thorburn, Archibald, *British Mammals*. Longmans, Green & Co., London, 1920–1; 2 vols. Contains 50 colour plates. The basis of the present book.

Thorburn, Archibald, *Game Birds and Wild-Fowl of Great Britain and Ireland*. Longmans, Green & Co., London, 1923. Contains 30 colour plates.

Thorburn, Archibald, *British Birds*. Longmans, Green & Co., London, 1925–6; 4 vols. Bibliographically the fourth edition of Thorburn (1915–18) with an octavo format and 192 new colour plates by the author.

Thorburn, Archibald, 'Kittiwakes nesting in Dunbar'. *Scot. Nat.* 1935 (212): 50. Thorburn's last published material and one of his few contributions to a scientific journal.

References Used by Thorburn

Baker, Sir Richard, *A Chronicle of the Kings of England*. London, 1643. This was published in many editions; Thorburn refers to one of 1650.

Barrett-Hamilton, Major see Hamilton

Beale, Thomas, *A Few Observations on the Natural History of the Sperm Whale*. Effingham Wilson, London, 1835. Quoted by Millais (1904–6).

Bell, Thomas, *A History of British Quadrupeds, including the Cetacea*. John Van Voorst, London, 1837. The second edition, to which Thorburn refers, was revised by the author with R. F. Tomes and E. R. Alston and published in 1874.

Blaine, Delabere Pritchett, *An Encyclopaedia of Rural Sports*. Longmans, Green & Co., London, 1840. This was reissued several times; Thorburn refers to an edition published in 1875.

Brown, J. A. Harvie and Buckley, Thomas Edward, *A Vertebrate Fauna of the Orkney Islands*. David Douglas, Edinburgh, 1891; vol. 4 of *The Vertebrate Fauna of Scotland*, 1887–1911; 11 vols.

Browne, George Forrest, *The Venerable Bede*. S.P.C.K., London; Pott, Young & Co., New York, 1879.

Kane, Elisha Kent, *Arctic Explorations in Search of Sir John Franklin*. T. Nelson & Sons, London, 1902. This appears to be the edition from which Thorburn's quotations are taken although one is not exact.

Hamilton, Gerald Edwin Hamilton Barrett [and Martin Alister Campbell Hinton], *A History of British Mammals*. Gurney & Jackson, London, 1910.

Harmer, Sir Sidney Frederic, K.B.E., *Report on Cetacea Stranded on the British Coasts During 1916*. British Museum (Natural History), London, 1917.

Harting, James Edmund, *British Animals Extinct Within Historic Times, With Some Account of British Wild White Cattle*. Trubner & Co., London, 1880.

Harting, James Edmund, *The Rabbit*. Longmans, Green & Co., London, 1898 (*Fur, Feather and Fin Series*).

Harvie Brown, J. A. see Brown

Hinton, Martin Alister Campbell, *Rats and Mice as the Enemies of Mankind*. British Museum, London, 2nd ed., 1920.

Millais, John Guille, *British Deer and Their Horns*. Sotheran & Co., London, 1897.

Millais, John Guille, *The Mammals of Great Britain and Ireland*. Longmans, Green & Co., London, 1904–6; 3 vols.

Murdoch, W. G. Burn, *Modern Whaling and Bear Hunting*. Seeley, Service & Co., London, 1917.

Pennant, Thomas, *British Zoology*. Warrington, London, 4th ed., 1776–77; 4 vols.

St John, Charles William George, *Wild Sports and Natural History of the Highlands*. T. N. Foulis, London and Edinburgh, new ed., 1919. This is not the 8th ed. referred to by Thorburn but contains the passages to which he refers.

Scammon, Charles Melville, *The Marine Mammals of the North-Western Coast of North America Described and Illustrated; Together With an Account of the American Whale-Fishery*. San Francisco (printed), New York, 1874.

Scoresby, William, the Younger, *An Account of the Arctic Regions, With a History and Description of the Northern Whale-Fishery*. Edinburgh, 1820; 2 vols.

Storer, John, *The Wild White Cattle of Great Britain*. Cassell, Petter & Calpin, London [1879].

Further Reading

Brink, F. H. van den, *A Field Guide to the Mammals of Britain and Europe*. Collins, London, 1967.

Burton, Maurice (ed.), *The Shell Natural History of Britain*. Michael Joseph, London, 1970.

Corbet, G. B., *The Identification of British Mammals*. British Museum (Natural History), London, 1964.

Crowcroft, P., *The Life of the Shrew*. Reinhardt, London, 1957.

Lawrence, M. J. and Brown, R. N., *Mammals of Britain, Their Tracks, Trails and Signs*. Blandford Press, London, 1973 (revised edition).

Matthews, L. H., *British Mammals*. Collins, London, 1952.

Page, F. J. T., *Field Guide to British Deer*. Mammal Society of the British Isles, 1957.

Phillips, W. A. A. and Blackmore, M., 'Mouse-eared Bats *Myotis myotis* in Sussex'. *Notes from the Mammal Society* no. 21, *J. Zool., Lond.* 1969; vol. 162, p. 4.

Racey, P. A. and Stebbings, R. E., 'Bats in Britain – A Status Report'. *Oryx*, 1972; vol. 11, no. 5, p. 319.

Sanders, E., *A Beast Book for the Pocket*. Oxford University Press, London, 1937.

Southern, H. N. (ed.), *The Handbook of British Mammals*, Blackwell, Oxford, 1964.

Stebbings, R. E., 'The Identification and Distribution of Bats of the Genus *Plecotus* in England'. *J. zoöl.*, London, 1967; vol. 153, p. 291.

Street, P., *Mammals in the British Isles*. Robert Hale, London, 1961.

Vesey-Fitzgerald, B., *British Bats*. Methuen, London, 1949.

Whitehead, G. K., *The Deer of Great Britain and Ireland*. Routledge and Kegan Paul, London, 1964.

Index